Whatever Happened to the Classroom Turtle?

How Animals Spark Student Engagement and a Love of Learning

BRADY BARR

Solution Tree | Press

Copyright © 2020 by Solution Tree Press

Materials here are copyrighted. All rights reserved. Readers may reproduce only those pages marked "Reproducible." Otherwise, no part of this book may be reproduced or transmitted in any form or by any means (electronic, photocopying, recording, or otherwise) without prior written permission of the publisher.

555 North Morton Street
Bloomington, IN 47404
800.733.6786 (toll free) / 812.336.7700
FAX: 812.336.7790

email: info@SolutionTree.com
SolutionTree.com

Visit **go.SolutionTree.com/instruction** to download the free reproducibles in this book.

Printed in the United States of America

Library of Congress Cataloging-in-Publication Data

Names: Barr, Brady, 1963- author.
Title: Whatever happened to the classroom turtle? : how animals spark student engagement and a love of learning / Brady Barr.
Description: Bloomington, IN : Solution Tree Press, [2020] | Includes bibliographical references and index.
Identifiers: LCCN 2019049391 (print) | LCCN 2019049392 (ebook) | ISBN 9781945349768 (paperback) | ISBN 9781945349775 (ebook)
Subjects: LCSH: Animals in education. | Children and animals. | Nature study.
Classification: LCC LB1044.9.A65 B37 2020 (print) | LCC LB1044.9.A65 (ebook) | DDC 371.33--dc23
LC record available at https://lccn.loc.gov/2019049391
LC ebook record available at https://lccn.loc.gov/2019049392

Solution Tree
Jeffrey C. Jones, CEO
Edmund M. Ackerman, President

Solution Tree Press

President and Publisher: Douglas M. Rife
Associate Publisher: Sarah Payne-Mills
Art Director: Rian Anderson
Managing Production Editor: Kendra Slayton
Production Editor: Alissa Voss
Content Development Specialist: Amy Rubenstein
Copy Editor: Evie Madsen
Text and Cover Designer: Abigail Bowen
Editorial Assistant: Sarah Ludwig

I dedicate this book to all the teachers in my life—past, present, formal, informal, and even those within my family. By far the most influential in my life were the teachers I had early on, in elementary school. Miriam Woods, Pauline Gough, Diane Williams, and Rita Sanders were all instrumental in shaping who I am today. Their dedication, understanding, and caring nature, along with their commitment and teaching style, sparked an interest deep inside of me for our natural world, which propelled me into my eventual career as a scientist for the National Geographic Society. Anyone that doesn't believe that teachers' efforts impact students lives is sorely mistaken. I am a living, breathing example of exactly that. Rarely a day goes by that I don't remember an incident, an action, or a word from these dedicated educators, and I am eternally grateful.

I would also like to dedicate this book to my parents, both educators in their own right. My mother was a public school librarian (I guess they call them media specialists now) for her entire career, and my father, a high school teacher, university professor, and eventually college dean. My mother is the smartest person on the planet, who always has exactly the right advice, suggestion, or encouraging words for every situation. She is one in a million. My father is responsible for my adventurous spirit and exploratory nature. He is up for anything, anywhere, and at any time, and he passed on this amazing mindset to me. Thanks, Mom and Dad—you're my rock!

Also, to my wife, Mei Len Sanchez-Barr, who was always there with support and guidance. She also proved to be an invaluable sounding board on all things animals and education. Her enthusiasm for hands-on education is only surpassed by her animal knowledge. She personifies exactly what this book is all about!

Acknowledgments

I would like to acknowledge all the teachers that inspired me to write this book, with their stories, anecdotes, experience, guidance, direction, and knowledge—most notably, Cale Morris. Cale is the finest example of a teacher that I know, one who champions hands-on learning with the countless animals in his classroom. His dedication to students is unparalleled. Through many conversations with Cale, this book was born. Teachers Paul Vandersteen, Rob Carmichael, and Paul Ritter were also extremely helpful. A shoutout goes to Eliza Geib, who helped me in a pinch with research. And, lastly, all the fine folks at Solution Tree, notably Amy Rubenstein and Alissa Voss, for putting up with me and making me sound like a real writer.

—Brady Barr

Solution Tree Press would like to thank the following reviewer:

Cristy Burt
Fourth-Grade Teacher
Sundance Elementary School
Los Lunas, New Mexico

Table of Contents

About the Author..........................xi

Introduction 1

CHAPTER 1
The Need for and Benefits of Animals in the Classroom..........................7
    Animals in the Classroom Benefit Students in the Classroom ... 8
    Animals in the Classroom Benefit Students Outside the Classroom 18
    Animals in the Classroom Have Real-World Benefits..........22
    Conclusion 23
    Cross-Curricular Lesson Ideas 25

CHAPTER 2
Hurdles to Animals in the Classroom 27
    Cost....................................29
    Daily Animal Care 31
    Animal Care During School Breaks 34
    Student Interactions With the Classroom Animal............37
    Liability and Safety Issues......................40
    Health Concerns 41
    Cultural Issues 42
    Teacher Work Overload 44
    Conclusion 45
    Cross-Curricular Lesson Ideas 46

CHAPTER 3
How to Select the Perfect Animal 49

- Student Preferences 50
- Allergies 51
- Age Appropriateness 51
- Life Span 52
- Need for Care During School Breaks 54
- Available Space 56
- Endangered Status 56
- Popular Classroom Pets 58
- Conclusion 58
- Cross-Curricular Lesson Ideas 61

CHAPTER 4
How to Locate Animals 65

- Sharing 65
- Adopting 67
- Fostering 69
- Buying 70
- Borrowing 71
- Conclusion 72
- Cross-Curricular Lesson Ideas 73

CHAPTER 5
How to Write Lesson Plans 75

- Natural Questions 75
- Inquiry-Based Lessons 76
- Online Resources 78
- Sample Lesson Plans for Researching, Selecting, and Adopting a Classroom Animal 78
- Conclusion 92

Epilogue 93

APPENDIX A
Tips..95
General Tips for Animals..................................... 95
Tips for Sourcing Food for Animals......................... 97
Tips for Finding, Setting Up, and Maintaining Cages
  and Aquariums.. 97

APPENDIX B
How to Create Self-Sustaining Food Sources for Your Classroom Animal..........99
How to Start a Fruit Fly Colony............................ 99
How to Start a Mealworm Colony............................101

References and Resources 105

Index 111

About the Author

Brady Barr, PhD, National Geographic's resident herpetologist, has dedicated his life to informing the public about the wonders of the natural world. Brady's hands-on style and engaging personality, combined with his breadth of scientific knowledge, allow him to bring the most exciting animals on the planet straight into people's living rooms.

Since 1997, Brady has traveled to more than eighty countries for National Geographic Television to host over one hundred wildlife documentaries—more than anyone in National Geographic's history. Notable television series he has hosted include *Crocodile Chronicles*, *Reptile Wild*, *Dangerous Encounters*, and *The Brady Barr Experience*.

Among his many notable achievements, Brady is the only person in history to capture and study all twenty-four species of crocodilians—a feat unlikely to ever be repeated, and one he uses to raise awareness for the plight of crocodilians everywhere.

The author of multiple, award-winning children's books about reptiles, Brady is also the star of the educational XBOX game *Dangerous Encounters*, a collaboration with Microsoft. On the research front, Brady has participated in studies with leading scientists throughout the world, including his ongoing research the National Geographic Society supports, into conservation of the American crocodile in Costa Rica, and his dietary study of alligators in the Florida Everglades.

Born in Fort Worth, Texas, and raised in Bloomington, Indiana, Brady earned a bachelor of science in education from Indiana University in 1987. He launched his teaching career at North Central High School in Indianapolis, Indiana, teaching subjects like zoology, biology, and earth and life sciences. With a highly interactive classroom style, Brady encouraged his students to "touch, see, and feel the animals firsthand." He went on to earn a master of science in 1994 and a PhD in biology from the University of Miami in 1997. In 2018, Brady received the Distinguished Alumni Award from Indiana University.

Among his many media appearances, Brady has appeared in the FOX Network Special *Supercroc* and logged multiple appearances on *The Tonight Show* with Jay Leno, *Oprah*, *The Today Show*, *The View*, and CNN. He's a frequent contributor to *National Geographic Kids* magazine, an ambassador for National Geographic's Young Explorers Program in Asia, and an educator and leader at the National Geographic Explorers Club for Kids. His speaking engagements include keynoting for the National Science Teachers Association, annual conventions of the International Congress of Zoology and Hoosier Association of Science Teachers, plus numerous schools, zoos, aquariums, museums, and fundraising events across the United States.

Brady is a member of the Endangered Species Coalition of the Council of State Governments and the International Crocodilian Specialist Group, and serves as a scientific expert for the International Union for Conservation of Nature and Natural Resources.

Brady and his wife, Mei Len Sanchez-Barr, a marine biologist and educator, cofounded and operate Eco Adventures (https://ecoadventures.org), a hands-on learning center for children in Maryland. They have two children.

To learn more about Brady's work, visit http://bradybarr.com. To book Brady Barr for professional development, contact pd@SolutionTree.com.

Introduction

Since 1997, I had what many would consider the dream job—that is, if you like exotic travel, animals, adventure, excitement, and even fame and fortune. I was a scientist for the National Geographic Society, and my job checked all of these boxes. I got to travel all over the world, ultimately touching down in over eighty countries, including many of the most remote, unexplored places on Earth. As National Geographic's resident animal expert, I had more wild adventures than you can shake a stick at—all filmed for television. I hosted over one hundred wildlife documentaries for National Geographic, appearing in network specials, three television series, and commercials. I was a regular on *The Tonight Show* with Jay Leno for many years, and a cartoon character in *National Geographic Kids* magazine (some say in real life as well). Microsoft even produced a Dr. Brady Barr XBOX Kinect video game. You know you've made it when you have your very own video game!

For me, a fanatical animal lover, this was a dream job because it entailed tangling with animals most people only dream about—everything from polar bears to platypuses, electric eels to elephants, and all critters in between—on a regular basis. For someone who loved travel as much as I did, it didn't get any better than this because expeditions took me from the most desolate stretches of the Sahara Desert to the most inhospitable areas of the African Congo, uncharted parts of the Amazon rainforest, forgotten corners of the Australian Outback, and even deep down into the abyss of the Atlantic Ocean. I saw it all as I wrangled dangerous critters in the name of science, education, and television.

Though it may have been my dream job, working as a National Geographic scientist did come with some drawbacks; anytime you interact up close and personal with dangerous animals, injuries can (and do) happen. My National Geographic film crew members would often say, "It's not *if* Brady gets hurt on an expedition, but *when*." Injuries just came with the territory, and after more than a handful of serious animal-inflicted injuries, I decided it was best for me to retire. Nowadays, I spend my time writing children's books and hitting the lecture circuit, where I speak to students and teachers about our natural world. Students and teachers are my favorite audience members because I'm still a kid at heart, and early on in my career, I too was a public school teacher. Before I was wrestling crocodiles in the swamp forests of Malaysia, I was wrestling the copy machine in the teachers' lounge at North Central High School in Indianapolis, Indiana, and trying to wrangle my students into the classroom where I taught biology. I truly loved my days as a teacher, though some were every bit as stressful as dealing with venomous snakes or wrestling angry crocodiles. While teaching, I really tried to make the world come alive for my students each and every day. I championed an interactive classroom.

Now when traveling the United States and speaking to teachers, I am asked many, many questions, but the most frequently asked is, "How did you get this dream job?" Folks always seem to think I grew up in some exotic locale, I was always the best and brightest student, or maybe I attended only the very best private schools or perhaps received special favors by knowing just the right influential people. The answer is *no*, for I had none of these things. I simply grew up the average kid of two hardworking parents, both educators, in an average southern Indiana town, and attended good public schools my entire childhood. What I did have were extremely dedicated teachers who championed inquiry-based, hands-on learning with classrooms filled with the wonders of nature. Yes, animals in the classroom! To these teachers I owe everything, and I dedicate this book to them.

So, how did it all begin? The year was 1970. As I did every morning, I walked to University Elementary School, across many busy streets and intersections, through neighborhoods, along railroad tracks, and through abandoned fields with my buddies, each of us with a brown-bag lunch in hand. After the routine trek to school on an average fall day seemingly like all the others, something happened that rocked my world and changed my life forever. I had taken my usual seat over by the window in Mrs. Woods's second-grade class—a seat I loved because that's where all the plants were, as well as many of the classroom animals. This classroom was amazing, especially through the eyes of a seven-year-old. It was filled with plants and animals, decorations on the walls, and mobiles hanging from the ceiling, all combining to create an ambiance that stimulated even the most disinterested students. I loved the place—it was like nothing I had ever seen before. Following the Pledge of Allegiance and morning announcements, Mrs. Woods began our day with something important: she wanted to select a student to be in charge of the classroom aquarium.

The aquarium was on the other side of the room over by the drinking fountain, and I could see it from my desk. I truly loved that thing! I marveled at how it was a magical little self-contained world. I didn't know it at the time, but it was actually just an average aquarium that you might find in any 1970s classroom. In fact, I think every classroom at my school had one, even the main office. It was standard ten gallons, made of thick glass with a heavy metal frame. Multicolored gravel was on the bottom, and in it stood a miniature statue of a bubbling deep-sea diver wearing a knife on his belt and holding a treasure chest. He held dominion over the handful of tropical fish that lazily swam about. A heater hung in the right-hand corner, with its glowing red eye letting you know it was actually working. In the other corner was a plastic box filled with angel hair filter floss and charcoal that kept the water nice and clean. A floating thermometer bobbed around the surface and an electric light on top illuminated this magical world, completing the setup. It truly was something to behold!

I was jolted to attention when I heard my name called as the student Mrs. Woods had chosen to be in charge of the aquarium. I just about fell out of my seat! *I* was the one selected to take care of this incredible little world: the snails, black mollies, swordtails, tetras, and angel fish. It was now my responsibility to keep the whole thing running. This was a game changer for a kid like me.

Over the course of my life, I have thought about that aquarium a lot. Was it a big deal for Mrs. Woods to put me, a seven-year-old, the new kid at school with no animal experience, in charge of a ten-gallon aquarium in the first semester of second grade? At the most basic level—no, not really. It was just an average aquarium, requiring little maintenance, but when I reflect back on it, that small aquarium changed my life. Initially, it made me somebody important—I was the guy who took care of the aquarium—but more important, it fostered a love and passion in me for our natural world I hadn't realized before, and it sparked an interest for animals and nature that catapulted me into a world that would eventually become my career as a National Geographic scientist. That aquarium changed my life. It was a big deal, a very big deal—a game changer!

The aquarium and I survived second grade. I moved on to third grade, and it stayed behind waiting for its next seven-year-old caretaker. My third-grade classroom also had an aquarium (though this one was without a diver), and the classroom was also home to a hermit crab, a lizard, and a guinea pig. Every year over the course of my grammar school career, it seemed I moved on to a different classroom, and more and different animals: praying mantis, crayfish, tadpoles, frogs, butterflies, salamanders, ant farms, lizards, hamsters, snakes, and even turtles! Ah, the classroom turtle. I think nearly every elementary school classroom had one, and some of even had multiple turtles. All these animals were wonderful additions, and the teachers, whether intended or not, incorporated all of them into just about everything we ever studied.

From social studies to mathematics to geography, it seemed like the animals were always a part of what we did, and we loved it.

The animals were not just part of my education but also my life, and it was the same for most students. I can remember countless family dinner conversations centered on something that happened with an animal at school. All the students experienced and learned through the animals' births, deaths, shedding, eating, growing, living, fighting, basking, breathing, and yes, even pooping. Did you know that a snail poops on top of its head? Well, all the third-graders in my class sure did because we watched the snails in our aquarium do it, and then we asked many questions about *how* and *why.* The animals in our classrooms were legendary, popular, and important. They were always there, each and every year, just like the desks, chalkboards, and American flag. They were literally part of our education, our daily routine, our lives.

Now I spend a great deal of time in U.S. classrooms, and they've changed a lot since I was a student. Chalkboards have been replaced by SMART Boards, film projectors and pull-down screens by tablets and computers, and wooden sticks by laser pointers. There are even high-tech security systems to simply get inside schools. All that stuff is pretty exciting; however, one thing I find that doesn't excite me and is all-too-disturbingly common, is the absence of animals in the classroom. Most classrooms I visit are completely devoid of life other than the students. No plants, no animals, no pooping snails . . . nothing. No aquarium, not even a classroom turtle! What happened? Whatever happened to the classroom turtle?

It's a complicated question to answer. I've spoken with a multitude of educators who say animals have disappeared due to a perplexing web of rules, regulations, laws, fears, liability issues, health concerns, paranoia, much more rigid curricula, teaching to the tests, and unfounded myths and legends. Let's use the lovable classroom turtle as an example. In the 1960s and 1970s, small turtles were all the rage. They were incredibly popular pets, and you could find them for sale not only in pet stores but also by mail order through ads in comic books and newspaper funnies, and at convenience stores, county fairs, carnivals, and of course your corner drugstore. They were often called *five-and-dime turtles* because so many were sold at variety stores. These stores sold thousands of small turtles, usually for less than a dollar, making them the first pet of many children and a popular staple in classrooms across America.

This would all change when, in 1975, the U.S. Food and Drug Administration (FDA) banned the sale of small turtles with shells less than four inches across, a very specific regulation that was a reaction to a health scare. The idea behind this ban was that small turtles could fit into the mouths of small children, thus increasing the risk of a bacterial infection, specifically salmonella, which is contracted orally. *Salmonella* is a common bacterium, and it is one of the most common causes of food poisoning. At the time, the FDA claimed the new rule would prevent thousands of children from contracting bacteria from turtles. However, it needs to be pointed out that salmonella bacteria are *not* unique to small turtles—in fact, not even unique to animals. Your pet dog at home can be harboring over fifty different types of salmonella. Further, children can just as easily contract salmonella in the school cafeteria as they can from the classroom turtle because it commonly turns up in foods. It can be found in chicken, eggs, tomatoes, milk, meat, juice, fruits, vegetables, breakfast cereals, peanuts, salsa, and chocolate, just to name a few. However, you can easily avoid the bacteria using reasonable precautions, such as good old-fashioned soap-and-water hand washing. Nonetheless, the 1975 law and accompanied hysteria, was the death knell for turtles, and they quickly all but disappeared from classrooms. Sadly, along with turtles, other animals started falling to the wayside as well. Classrooms were purging their beloved guinea pigs, finches, hamsters, crayfish, and other critters. The reasons were many, not just the bacteria scare but also everything from unfounded paranoia, increased liability risks, potential problems for children with allergies, People for the Ethical Treatment of Animals (PETA) protests, and even a much more rigidly structured curriculum led to many school districts to decide that, sadly, there just wasn't any place for classroom animals anymore.

The following pages highlight the many benefits your students can receive from animals in the classroom and outline potential hurdles you might come up against. Most important, I will describe how to navigate these "speed bumps." I have gathered some useful, and sometimes funny, stories from teachers and from my own experience—these are included in the book as Tales From the Front Lines. I have also sprinkled some quotes from teachers and students throughout the book about their experiences with animals in the classroom. At the end of each chapter, I include Cross-Curricular Lesson Ideas to provide a catalyst for lessons connecting your classroom animal and various class subjects. To conclude the book, appendices A and B provide a compilation of helpful tips for all kinds of animals, including tips for sourcing food and maintaining cages and enclosures. If you are a K–12 teacher, you have come to the right place! I will put your fears to rest and give you all the answers you need so you too can enjoy the countless rewards of classroom animals and possibly launch kids like me into their eventual careers as explorers, conservationists, TV personalities, or world-class scientists. Long live the classroom turtle!

CHAPTER 1

The Need for and Benefits of Animals in the Classroom

Society is producing children who are often out of touch with nature. Almost on a weekly basis, I am amazed to come across children who have never clutched a crayfish, touched a frog, or held a snail. With the advent of the internet, smartphones, tablets, virtual reality, and video games, children spend the majority of their free time indoors, increasingly disconnected from nature. Even air-conditioning has played a role in children losing touch with nature. In the past, the sounds of nature surrounded people's lives. With windows open, children would wake to the sounds of songbirds in the morning, go to sleep to the call of crickets or frogs, and listen to the din of cicadas throughout the day. In journalist and author Richard Louv's powerful 2005 book, *Last Child in the Woods*, he cites U.S. Census Bureau data when he recalls that in the early 1900s, most folks kept their windows open, with only 12 percent of homes having air-conditioning. By 1970, the figure was over 70 percent, and by 2001, almost 80 percent of U.S. homes had air-conditioning (as cited in Louv, 2005). This increasingly commonplace occurrence of air-conditioning has changed much of children's ability to interact with animal life and nature, due to shuttered windows and, with them, the sounds of the outside world.

You may want to sit down for this next statistic: a 2016 survey reveals that U.S. children spend less time outside experiencing nature than do prison inmates (as cited in Martinko, 2016). According to journalist Katherine Martinko (2016), maximum security prisoners in the United States get a required two hours outdoors daily while half the children worldwide spend less than an hour outside. Things have really gotten bad when incarcerated prisoners are experiencing more nature than our children! In addition, findings show children lack good general knowledge about animals and other natural organisms. For instance, researchers at the University of Cambridge (Blamford, Clegg, Coulson, & Taylor, 2002) find that typical eight-year-olds are better at identifying Pokémon characters than real-life organisms, with almost 80 percent accuracy for Pokémon animals and less than 50 percent for real organisms.

> "I am continually amazed at the lack of experience today's kids have with animals. I will bring out a common animal, like a box turtle, and they just go bonkers, like it's the greatest thing they've ever seen. It's incredibly rewarding, but also sad on so many levels, that these kids have zero experience with common backyard animals."
>
> —JESSICA ROSNICK, *educator, Maryland*
> *(personal communication, February 11, 2018)*

This is why I argue that animals in the classroom have never been more important. Due to changes in the built environment, advances in technology, and other factors beyond their control, children simply aren't experiencing nature the way they used to—and this is affecting their learning. In this chapter, I discuss research and life experiences that show how having animals in the classroom benefits students both inside and outside the classroom, and can even have a powerful and permanent impact on the children's wider communities.

Animals in the Classroom Benefit Students in the Classroom

Research shows animals in the classroom can have a profound effect on student outcomes—behavioral, emotional, and academic. Studies also demonstrate how animals play an important role in our lives even before we reach school age. A Rutgers University and University of Virginia research project finds that toddlers prefer live animals to toys, when given a choice (Smith & Bowater, 2012). The implication is that children have a predisposition or natural affinity for animals from an early age. It's no coincidence that a great deal of children's television programs and books are dominated by animal characters. Children have an innate interest in animals from the get-go, so it just makes sense to continue to use animals as examples throughout their education to stimulate learning. Animals, therefore, play an important role in learning and development—further evidence that educators should include animals in the classroom to facilitate instruction.

> "The bottom line is that in today's world, children and adults are totally disconnected with nature. I'll bring out a red-tailed hawk for the students to see and half the kids say that it is a chicken. It's just unreal. We have to get today's kids reconnected with nature, and what better way to do it than having a classroom animal!"
> —**ROB CARMICHAEL,** *educator, Illinois*
> *(personal communication, November 2, 2018)*

When children do start school, it can be an anxious, stressful time. It sure was for me. Luckily, many children find animals in the classroom to have a calming effect. I don't think it is an accident that so many dentists' and doctors' offices have aquariums in the waiting room. Something as simple as the rhythmic stream of bubbles from an aquarium filter can be soothing for a nervous, scared child (Futterman, 2015). For these children, animals in the classroom can be a game changer.

Many of you do have, or will have, students with special needs in your classrooms. It's estimated that around six million students, or about 13 percent of the U.S. school population, is made up of special needs students (Poth, 2018). These kids process the world around them a little differently than other students and may have to deal with social, behavioral, or emotional challenges. Animals in the classroom can help alleviate or manage these challenges. Studies have long found the benefits of animals in helping children with emotional and social issues, finding that animals decrease behavioral problems and anxiety while increasing appropriate social behaviors (Bueche, 2003; Fine, 2010; Newlin, 2003; Ormerod, Edney, Foster, & Whyman, 2005; Raup, 2002). I am sure that many of you may have found comfort stroking a cat or hugging a dog in times of sorrow, or have soothingly watched fish swim about in an aquarium during times of anxiety. Much in the same way that these animal interactions help adults, they can also help certain students cope with their feelings and classroom anxiety—especially those students with special needs. Jennifer Porche, a special education teacher in Alabama, summed up her experiences with Buddy, her classroom guinea pig:

> We have many moments of frustration and sensory overload that often lead to meltdowns within our classroom setting. Buddy has helped so many of our students feel better when they get to just sit and read to him. (Pets in the Classroom, 2016)

Another teacher describes how Charlie, his classroom bearded dragon, benefits his students with special needs:

> I have a couple of autistic students, and Charlie often sits with them and helps them on days when things are out of sorts. . . . The biggest success story for Charlie is that we have a student in an emotional/behavioral class who has a really hard time fitting in. He gets very angry at times, and when teachers aren't able to calm him down with the usual strategies, we find just holding and talking to Charlie for a few minutes when he gets upset works every time. It's like a small miracle. (Pets in the Classroom, 2016)

Tales From the Front Lines
My Salamander Just Grew a New Leg!

A teacher from Delaware shared a powerful story with me. Ms. D. had a student with a disability: he was missing one of his hands, and he was very self-conscious about it. He was a withdrawn, shy, and retiring kid, and he avoided interaction with anyone. He wouldn't participate in class, even though he was a bright kid, and he avoided attention at all cost. His parents and teachers had tried many things to get the boy to open up, but nothing had worked—until he arrived in Ms. D.'s classroom.

Ms. D.'s room was host to a number of animals, including a tank of aquatic salamanders. One of the salamanders in the tank was missing most of one of its legs from an unfortunate run-in with a hungry turtle. (Note: Never keep turtles and aquatic salamanders in the same tank!) Ms. D. thought the poor salamander might die, but amazingly it healed, survived the injury, and in fact became one of the more active salamanders in the tank, despite living life with just three legs.

Life went on until the holiday break, at which point something special started happening with the disabled salamander. One day after the break, while gazing into the tank of salamanders, a student noticed something remarkable: it looked like the salamander had a new leg, or was at least in the process of growing a new leg! The entire class was fascinated by this discovery, but one student in particular was more interested than the others—the student with the missing hand.

Later that day, after school had ended, the boy came to speak to the teacher—something that had never happened before. He said that he had many questions about the salamander and wanted to talk. Ms. D. and the boy talked at length about many things, not just the salamander, and she saw a side of the boy that had never been revealed. She encouraged him to do some research and learn more about axolotls and what had happened. The boy became keenly interested in the power of regeneration—the regrowing of lost body parts—which is an ability held by many animals. He discovered that some animals could not only regrow limbs but also actual organs like the heart or even their brain!

He became an expert on the subject, but more importantly, it brought him out of his shell. He gave the class a presentation of his findings, about how the process works, which animals have the ability, and even the potential for human applications. His classmates had many questions as well, and he actually interacted with them, answering their questions as best he could. Ms. D. said the most amazing thing was that this shy, withdrawn kid, who normally wouldn't even make eye contact with anyone, actually stood in front of his classmates and spoke to them. He was now the go-to guy for all things salamander. He had a made a real, meaningful connection with this classroom animal. Though he was still self-conscious about his disability, it was not anywhere near as extreme as before he connected with the salamanders. That small classroom salamander and its amazing power of regeneration changed that student in ways that Ms. D. just couldn't describe.

It's clear that animals have a calming effect on kids, especially those who process the world around them differently. Further, animals can energize and engage special needs students that may be withdrawn, shy, or retiring. As a result, animals can be like therapeutic gold in your classroom, helping you assist your special needs students!

Further, having access to animals in the classroom is a tremendous and valuable source of hands-on learning. When compared to written or computer-based instruction, students learn concepts faster and retain knowledge longer when teachers utilize hands-on learning (Freeman et al., 2014). I cannot tell you how many times I sat in a classroom fighting off the urge to fall asleep as a speaker droned on and on in a seemingly endless lecture. Of course, I didn't learn a thing; I spent most of that time daydreaming. When we as humans are bored, our brain does something about it. It sends that feeling, that information, to a part of the brain that does one of three things: (1) ignores it, (2) fights against it as a negative experience, or (3) avoids it (for example, through daydreaming; Willis, 2015). The solution to this problem is engagement through *active learning methods.* One meta-analysis of over 225 studies that focused on lecturing versus hands-on learning methods found that active learning increases exam scores by 6 percent, which ultimately led the researchers to conclude that active learning should be the preferred teaching method in classrooms (Freeman et al., 2014). Further, Bajak (2014) finds that students learning primarily through the lecture method are 1.5 times more likely to fail than students that are taught by more stimulating active learning methods. Active learning methods go by many names, including *hands-on learning, experiential learning* (learning through experience), or *kinesthetic learning* (using one's body to touch and sense things), but all involve learning by *doing*, not just passively listening.

While many studies have shown the benefits of hands-on learning, fewer have specifically investigated hands-on learning with animals. However, in my experience, active learning methods involving animals are likely to be particularly engaging and memorable for students. I still vividly remember many hands-on labs and activities I took part in with live animals during my formative years. I remember the crayfish and how it moved, the earthworm and how it responded to light and dark, and even the clam and how it responded to colored water. In my opinion, there simply isn't any better example than a living, breathing entity to illustrate the power of hands-on learning. I have seen many a student grasp concepts and retain knowledge better while holding a squirming snake or other critter than while simply sitting and listening to a teacher. And, this potential for hands-on engagement is multidisciplinary. A biology lesson may ask why snakes are covered in scales as the student examines the scales firsthand. A geography lesson may require students to explain where a particular creature is located on a map. For a dynamic mathematics lesson, a teacher may ask students to measure the length of a snake (not an easy task when the critter is wriggling and writhing!) or to calculate its change in weight over time. In each case, such hands-on learning excites the senses, invigorates emotions, and activates the brain. The student holding the animal might be excited, ecstatic, reluctant, or proud, or he or she may have questions, thoughts, or memories relating to the animal. When this happens, the amygdala in the brain produces a neurochemical enhancement—like a memory chip—that improves the staying power of the information learned during the lesson (Willis, 2015). This means that fun, engaging, hands-on activities lead to information being retained longer than it usually would be. Active learning methods such as holding or interacting with animals also tend to activate both sides of the brain—both the visual and spatial half (the right side) and the listening and analyzing half (the left side). When both sides of the brain are activated, the brain forms more powerful connections and is able to store more information for eventual recall (Semrud-Clukeman, n.d.; Willis, 2015). The neuroscience is clear, and our real-world experiences back it up: learning is more engaging and concepts are more easily retained when students are involved in hands-on learning. It's time to get animals back into classrooms!

> "I have animals in the classroom because I discovered long ago that it is an exciting way to engage students and allow them to have a hands-on part of working with various species. My students raise animals, collect data, and reintroduce endangered species back into the wild! When kids are finished with my class, they may not focus their future energy on a particular species that they worked with in my classroom, but I have found that they do transfer their energy to whatever animal they are passionate about inside or outside of the classroom."
>
> —**PAUL RITTER,** *high school ecology teacher, Illinois*
> *(personal communication, January 2, 2018)*

It is also notable that including animals in the classroom has been given a big, thumbs-up seal of approval from science teachers themselves. The National Science Teachers Association (NSTA, 1991), the largest organization of science teachers on the planet with close to sixty thousand members, firmly supports animals in the classroom. NSTA's (1991) *Guidelines for Responsible Use of Animals in the Classroom* states, "Observation and experimentation with living organisms give students unique perspectives of life processes that are not provided by other modes of instruction. Studying animals in the classroom enables students to develop skills of observation and comparison, a sense of stewardship and an appreciation for the unity, interrelationships, and complexity of life" (p. 244). Further, the NSTA 2008 position statement says student interaction with organisms is one of the most effective ways to achieve many of the goals outlined in the National Science Education Standards (NSES; as cited in National Research Council [NRC], 1996). The NSES are the NRC-formulated science education guidelines for K–12 students in North American schools. Having animals in the classroom aligns with the NSES guidelines, most notably the Science as Inquiry standards (as cited in NRC, 1996; see figure 1.1, page 14).

- Understanding of scientific concepts.
- An appreciation of "how we know" what we know in science.
- Understanding of the nature of science.
- Skills necessary to become independent inquirers about the natural world.
- The dispositions to use the skills, abilities, and attitudes associated with science.

Source: NRC, 1996, p. 105.

Figure 1.1: NSES Science as Inquiry standards.

In addition, the National Association of Biology Teachers (NABT, 2019) is on board with animals in the classroom. In its mission statement, the NABT Board of Directors (2019) encourages live animals in the classroom, stating that the responsible use of animals in biological education is essential to the understanding of life on Earth.

"I've always been animal crazy, but my high school didn't allow classroom animals, so I volunteered at a local learning center that did. My time spent there working with various critters changed my life. I am now living my dream in veterinary school at Virginia Tech University. I'm going to work with animals the rest of my life!"

—**SIERRA RUBIN,** *veterinary student, Virginia (personal communication, August 14, 2018)*

In addition to large organizations such as NSTA and NABT recognizing the benefits of animals in the classroom, many research studies detail the positive effects animals have on the classroom experience that, simply put, make it a better place for all. Anyone who has spent any time in a classroom will attest to how important it is for teachers to decrease bad behavior, increase class participation, instill compassion and respect for others, have a calming influence, and decrease stress and anxiety in students. You would likely be hard-pressed to find any teacher who wouldn't agree as to how instrumental these elements are in running a productive and positive classroom; in fact, you could consider them keystones when building the ideal classroom. Notably, numerous studies show having animals in the classroom has direct benefits in addressing these elements (American Humane Association [AHA], 2015; Arcken, 1989; Blue, 1986; Daly & Suggs, 2010; Mars Petcare US, 2017; McCardle, McCune, Griffin, Esposito, & Freund, 2011; Melson, 2001; Sack, 2003).

To expound on the findings of one of those studies, 1,200 North American teachers identify the following six specific, positive effects of animals in the classroom (AHA, 2015). They:

1. Increase students' responsibility and leadership
2. Increase students' compassion, empathy, and respect
3. Enhance and enrich a variety of traditional academic lessons
4. Decrease stress
5. Increase student comfort levels, making them more engaged
6. Expose students to new experiences and opportunities

All these wonderful outcomes are easily achievable. And remember, over 1,200 teachers themselves relay these positive effects. The simple act of incorporating animals into the classroom has a positive impact on teachers as well.

Another study illustrated this very thing: how animals aren't just for classroom fun, but how they also have a very positive impact on the kids inside the classroom. The research identified three key areas of positive improvement: (1) behavioral impact, (2) social interaction, and (3) attitude improvement (Mars Petcare U.S., 2017). When animals were present, children more responsibly followed directions, asked more pertinent questions, and displayed better engagement overall. Furthermore, the students were less fidgety and more attendant in classrooms with animals, and their attitudes toward school were improved as evident by displays of greater respect, empathy, and responsibility (Mars Petcare US, 2017).

> "There's no more powerful tool than using animals for education. They teach us so much, and I think that the schools that are open to allowing animals see students acting more engaged, getting better grades, and becoming more motivated."
> —**TONI CARMICHAEL,** *high school teacher, Illinois*
> *(personal communication, May 22, 2018)*

At the simplest level, most studies find that animals in the classroom just make learning more fun (American Humane Association, 2015; Arcken, 1989; Blue, 1986; Daly & Suggs, 2010; Mars Petcare U.S., 2017; McCardle et al., 2011; Melson, 2001; Sack, 2003). In my experience, incorporating live animals into classroom instruction can have a magical effect. They stimulate learning, making it exciting, real, tangible, and fresh. Cale Morris, a middle school teacher in Mesa, Arizona, saw this firsthand in an experiment he devised and carried out with two of his seventh-grade science classes. For a lab involving animals, Cale allowed one class to interact with live animals, but gave only photos of the very same animals to the other class. Cale took notes and observed the students while they completed the lab assignment. As Cale describes, the results were dynamic:

> The two classes stood in stark contrast to each other. The class with live animals was a frenzy of excitement, and the students were visibly happy and enthusiastic to do the lab, with all on task discussing the animals. The other class, using only animal photos, was quiet, disinterested, and talking about topics that did not relate to science—things like their favorite music artist or what their weekend plans were. (C. Morris, personal communication, April 6, 2019)

The students in both classes used the information they gathered to complete a lab report, and unsurprisingly, the class with live animals scored dramatically higher on the lab exercise as well as the unit quiz. The class without live animals had only one student ask a single question throughout the entire lab, whereas the class with live animals had nonstop questions—an important element in the learning process. Cale concludes by saying, "It was crystal clear to me that using living organisms provided a richer learning experience for students, and that experience helps them better retain the knowledge they gain."

Tales From the Front Lines

Turtle Toes

Along with my wife (marine biologist Mei Len Sanchez-Barr), I own and operate a hands-on learning center—Eco Adventures (https://ecoadventures.org)—for kids in the state of Maryland. It's a simulated two-story rainforest filled with vines and trees, and even outfitted with a lagoon with live crocodiles and turtles swimming around. It has giant tortoises wandering the facility, and loads of lizards, snakes, fish, frogs, mammals, and other animals call it home. This place is all about kids and animals, and designed so the two can get up close and personal with each other—a hands-on heaven if you're a kid like me. We have many children experience Eco Adventures every day through school field trips, home school classes, after-school care, or simply for open play. One day in 2010, a large school group was visiting and I was talking about the wildlife of the Chesapeake Bay. At the time, I was talking about turtles, and I had an endangered diamondback terrapin out for the students to interact with. One student raised her hand and asked about another turtle found in the bay. The student saw that we had a very large snapping turtle in the rainforest lagoon, and she wanted to know more about it. I ran through all sorts of facts and figures about the diamondback terrapin and how important it was to the health of the Chesapeake Bay, but that didn't seem to satisfy her. She had a specific question, an important question, one that she just had to know the answer to: How many toes does a snapping turtle have? Man, it was a great question! I told her that I could give her the answer but that she would probably forget it by the time she had dinner. However, if she was willing to take off her shoes, roll up her pant legs, muster up some courage, wade into the rainforest lagoon—avoiding the curious crocodiles—and carefully help me capture the big old snapping turtle, she could count the toes herself. Doing it that way, I promised her that she would never forget the answer. At the urging of her frenzied classmates she agreed, and in front of her entire class she waded in, wrestled with that big snapper, and got an accurate count of its toes. She was a hero in the eyes of her teachers and classmates, especially some of the boys.

Many years passed, and that little girl is now in veterinary school. Not long ago, she stopped by the facility just to say hello. It was great to see her all grown up, and I asked her if she remembered how many toes a snapping turtle has. Without missing a beat, she told me, and then went on to say what a powerful experience it was and how in many ways it changed her life!

I still have that big snapper, and since that day long ago with the little girl, many, many, kids have rolled up their pants and waded on in to count the toes.

Animals in the Classroom Benefit Students Outside the Classroom

I like to think of classroom animals just as I do about taking a multivitamin each day: they are good for everyone, and they make the world a healthier, happier place. Animals in the classroom not only help kids inside the classroom; the benefits carry over into their home life as well. Studies have shown that experiential learning with animals in the classroom better equips students to deal with life. The WALTHAM study (Mars Petcare U.S., 2017) emphasizes that students exposed to animals in the classroom were able to make friends more easily and to more calmly deal with conflicts. Another study (American Humane Association, 2015) found that children involved with animals displayed more empathy, compassion, and respect for others. Furthermore, being around animals better equips children to fight off infections by improving their immune systems (American Humane Association, 2015). Healthy children means increased attendance in school, which is something all teachers can appreciate. An Australian study (Herbert & Lynch, 2017) highlighted how animals in the classroom can provide opportunities for students to connect with their communities—whether it be by fostering interest in museums, public libraries, zoos, aquariums, and pet stores; by providing topics of discussion for children to share with friends and family when not in school (like telling Grandpa all about the way the snake shed its skin!); or through enabling community communication through blogs, neighborhood newsletters, or media. So, take your multivitamin and experience animals in the classroom every day! It will help make the world a better place.

"Classroom discipline problems just dropped off the radar since I started including live animals and involving students as much as possible in the animals' care and maintenance. Seems like my popularity has mysteriously risen as well!"

—**KIRSTEN SHARP-GOLDEN,** *elementary teacher,* Texas
(personal communication, December 28, 2018)

Further, a focus on social and emotional learning (SEL) is sweeping through districts across America. Table 1.1 illustrates how engaging students with classroom pets can support SEL.

Wow, it's like the benefit of having animals in the classroom is that children can ultimately become better human beings, not just better students in the classroom. Students will receive the benefits of enhanced reading, writing, and storytelling skills, as well as an overall increased interest in learning, but the parents, teachers, and peers

Table 1.1: How Classroom Animals Support Student SEL

SEL Competencies	Description of Competencies	Examples of How Animals in the Classroom Support SEL Competencies
Self-Awareness and Goal Setting	Animals evoke a lot of different emotions and responses for humans. Setting goals will help students identify their emotions and control their behavior.	Students set goals for the following. • How they will respond to the animal • What the classroom animal can teach them (For example, putting the animal's needs before their own, determining what they need to provide for the animal, and so on.)
Self-Management and Goal Achievement	Students regulate their own emotions, behaviors, and learning to achieve both personal and academic goals.	Students do the following. • Interact and spend time with the animal. • Improve the animal's life within the classroom. • Learn from the animal.
Social Awareness and Empathy	Students support classmates with their own self-awareness and goal setting, as well as gain a better understanding for the classroom animal's needs through their peers.	Students do the following. • Gain awareness of how the animal impacts their own feelings, emotions, and learning. • Understand the animal's needs. • Identify others' needs, especially students struggling with self-management, and become a positive influencer by modeling appropriate animal care.
Relationship Skills, Teamwork, and Collaboration	Students communicate clearly, demonstrate active listening, and resist poor choices by negotiating conflict constructively.	Students do the following. • Understand the needs of the classroom animal are a team priority. • Focus on group, not individual, outcomes based on the experiences and learning through the classroom animal. • Recognize others' strengths through teamwork and collaboration on animal-related learning and tasks.
Responsible Decision Making	Students care about the well-being of their peers, the teacher, and the classroom animal by demonstrating constructive, positive, and safe choices.	Students do the following. • Understand they all have a similar goal (namely, the well-being of the animal). • Exhibit better self-control and self-regulation as a result of having goals and self-awareness. • Deliberately and purposefully take care of and learn about the classroom animal, as a result of greater connections to themselves and the class as a whole.

reap the benefits as well as the student improves in self-management and self-awareness, social awareness, empathy, and relationship skills. Everything from enriching responsibility to encouraging nurturing; building self-esteem, compassion, and respect; increasing social interactions; and decreasing stress and anxiety are all benefits of animals in the classroom. Gail Melson, in her book *Where the Wild Things Are: Animals in the Lives of Children*, points out, "Kindness curricula—teaching respect for animals, humans, and the environment—are finding their way into many school systems, driven by the rising tide of school-based violence" (Melson, 2001, p. 193). As many educators are discovering, animals can and do change lives.

Tales From the Front Lines
Bully and the Bullfrog

An elementary school teacher in Tampa, Florida, witnessed a perfect example of how animals in the classroom can impact kids. Mrs. M. told me that there was one student at her school that everyone knew about—all the students, staff, administrators, everyone—because, well, he was a big-time bully. This kid seemed to always be in trouble for something. Fighting, stealing, talking back, being disrespectful and defiant—you name it, this student had done it. It seemed like he had a permanent seat outside the principal's office. At the beginning of the school year, Mrs. M. gasped out loud when she saw this student's name on her class roster, knowing she was going to have her hands full.

The school year started and, as expected, the student was a problem, constantly harassing and bullying the other children. He also was frequently absent from class because he would often start his days by bullying kids outside the building and end up in the principal's office before instruction even began. It was clear that something had to change. The principal stopped by Mrs. M.'s classroom one afternoon to discuss an idea he had to keep the student out of trouble. He asked if Mrs. M. would be willing to let the boy hang out inside her classroom each morning instead of waiting outside, where he seemed to get into the most trouble.

Mrs. M. agreed, and she and the boy decided that he would help take care of the classroom animals before school. She thought that changing water, feeding the animals, and cleaning the cages might keep him out of trouble, and she also knew from her experience that working with the classroom animals could have an effect on self-control, compassion, and pride—all things that could benefit the bully.

At first the student didn't always show up. However, as time went by, he became more and more reliable. He took a particular liking to the classroom bullfrog. As time passed, he started showing up each morning with an empty soda can full of cockroaches that he had captured at home the night before. The bullfrog loved eating those roaches! The other students started asking the bully about the roaches and the frog, and, surprisingly, he began to respond to them, answering their questions, giving feeding demonstrations, and sharing information. The bullying in class all but disappeared over the next few months as the student became more and more involved with the classroom animals. Some of his previous teachers heard about the change and stopped by the classroom to see for themselves. One morning the principal himself even showed up and sat down with the bully for a frog feeding demonstration and a chat. Afterwards, he pulled Mrs. M. aside and said how this student's behavior change was one of the most dramatic that he had ever seen in his many years at the school. As the principal left the room, he turned back to Mrs. M., paused, and said, "Maybe we should require all the classrooms to have bullfrogs!"

Animals in the Classroom Have Real-World Benefits

In addition to benefitting students inside the classroom, animals in the classroom reap dramatic, large-scale, real-world results as well. As an example, in 1999, crocodile expert Juan Bolanos asked me to help implement a crocodile Head Start program in Costa Rica. This program takes animals at the beginning of their life, raises them in captivity for a short period of time, and then releases them into the wild later when they are bigger, thus giving them a head start on life. The premise is that the larger the animal is when released into the wild, the greater its chances for survival. When crocodiles are very small, many other animals use them as a food source, but as they get larger, they have fewer and fewer predators. So, the larger the crocodiles when released, the higher their survivorship in the wild.

Beyond this natural danger to baby crocodiles is a specific threat from humans in this specific area. The backstory is that American crocodiles were being illegally hunted at an alarming rate in a particular river in Costa Rica. The local fishermen believed the crocodiles were eating all the fish in the river—the very fish residents relied on to survive. However, the crocs were on their way to extinction. To compound this looming catastrophe, the crocodiles were also considered a *keystone species*, meaning the health of the entire ecosystem could rely on their presence. Conservationists, scientists, local police, and government officials all came to the aid of the crocodiles. Signs were placed all along the river informing the public the crocodiles were protected by law. Increased law enforcement patrols, community seminars, and incentive programs were all enacted, but nothing seemed to help. The croc killing continued, and nothing seemed to work. It looked as if the croc population—and therefore possibly the entire ecosystem—was doomed. However, at the eleventh hour, a crocodile biologist and local educator had an idea: start a crocodile head-start program in schools along the river.

The program operated like this: trained biologists collected crocodile eggs from wild nests along the river. These eggs were then provided to classrooms, where the students and teachers were taught how to build incubators and care for them. Wildlife biologists and other experts gave lectures to the students, educating them about the life history, biology, and importance of the local crocs. After a number of weeks, the eggs hatched and the students were tasked with taking care of the baby crocs until the end of the year. When the school year ended, all the children took their baby crocs to the river and released them into the wild, thus repopulating the ecosystem with the valuable species.

The project was a huge success, and the illegal killing all but ended. When the students would say goodbye and release their crocs into the wild, they were sad, with many even weeping as they waved goodbye. That's because they came to love these misunderstood creatures. The project fostered a love and understanding of crocs that ran deep in these students, and that is what saved the crocs. The poachers were the students' parents, extended families, friends, and town folk, but once the students felt ownership over the reptiles, they became very protective. They worked hard to convince their families and friends not to kill the crocs, and this method proved effective. With the illegal killing effectively stopped, the crocodile numbers increased to historic levels. This was partly due to the head start the students gave the animals but mostly due to people's changed attitudes. The crocodiles were no longer looked at as unimportant and something to destroy. The students, now armed with knowledge, facts, and personal experience, discovered a newfound passion they used effectively to change the attitudes of the local adults—the poachers. The students and the crocodiles in the head-start program saved the local crocodile population, making a real-world difference.

As I travel and retell this success story to educators, it has inspired dedicated teachers to spawn many new and different head-start programs. It doesn't have to be crocodiles; other suitable living organisms include butterflies, clams, sea grasses, turtles, frogs, and snakes—whatever species is of special concern in a particular geographic area. A teacher I know started a head-start program for alligator snapping turtles outside Chicago, a species essentially extinct in northern Illinois. His students played a valuable role in helping to bring back this forgotten turtle in local waterways. This program is a great way for students to see how their efforts with animals in the classroom can make a real difference in the world we live in.

> "We raised terrapins in class and then let them go into the Bay. It was sad to say goodbye, but now I know that I want to be a marine biologist!"
> —**BRADY J.,** *third-grade student, Maryland*
> *(personal communication, October 10, 2019).*

Conclusion

Considering the multitude of notable positive effects animals in the classroom have on students and teachers—from calming emotions to increasing retention, and engaging with the local community to even assisting with conservation projects—

the question seems not to be, Why should we have animals in our classrooms? but rather, How can we afford *not* to have animals in our classrooms? Research projects, graduate theses, collaborative studies, anecdotal evidence, real-life stories, scientific findings, and good common sense all overwhelmingly show the benefits of simply inviting animals into the student experience. In addition to convincing you, the reader, of the considerable benefits, the information this chapter provides is also helpful when coming up against reluctant administrators or department heads who see little or no benefit of animals in the classroom. In the next chapter, I discuss some of the hurdles you may face to including animals in your classroom.

Cross-Curricular Lesson Ideas

Social Studies and Civics
Unfortunately, during times of war, wildlife can become casualties. Studies show a direct correlation between war and animal deaths (Hanson et al., 2009).

Invite your students to conduct research of their own on how government conflicts led to a rise in poaching or a loss of habitat for animals on the endangered species list. Students may want to take action by learning more about and supporting organizations such as the Wildlife Justice Commission (https://wildlifejustice.org/work-with-us).

Geography
Have students study animals native to their local area and learn about why these animals live in that particular habitat. Perhaps consider having them research careers that work with these animals and the impact these workers have had on helping the animal population.

Art and Science
Have students draw, paint, or create a model of the life cycle of a local animal and its habitat. Younger students may use feathers, snakeskins, or other textured items to create the texture of animals' coverings or animal tracks in clay.

Photography
Challenge students to conduct an assignment photographing various populations with animals. They could choose elderly populations, young children, people with disabilities, and so on. Have them photograph the interactions of these populations with animals.

CHAPTER 2
Hurdles to Animals in the Classroom

Although the evidence is clear—animals in- and outside the classroom are beneficial to students, teachers, and communities—it is wise to prepare; not everyone is going to think having animals in your classroom is a great idea. And even if you encounter a surprisingly supportive cohort of stakeholders, there will inevitably be some hurdles to actually getting the animal in your classroom and considering its ongoing care. In this chapter, I highlight a few of the hurdles you and your students are likely to encounter and provide guidance on how to work through them.

Let's begin with what teachers feel are the greatest obstacles to having animals in the classroom. The American Humane Association (2015) study involving 1,200 teachers seems like a great place to begin. The participating teachers report numerous and varied obstacles to their pursuit of having animals in the classroom. Figure 2.1 (page 28) breaks down those obstacles by frequency.

An initial look over this list may lead you to think, "Maybe I don't need or want animals in the classroom after all." I would advise you not to be overwhelmed. Animals in the classroom are beneficial, and managing these hurdles is doable. In my experience, just about every obstacle can be overcome using one of two strategies: (1) reasonable precautions and (2) reasonable judgement. In this section, I will discuss several of these obstacles and how to overcome them in greater detail. I elaborate on the following topics.

- Cost
- Daily animal care
- Animal care during school breaks

28 WHATEVER HAPPENED TO THE CLASSROOM TURTLE?

Challenge	Percent
Incurring additional costs for the pet (beyond grant money)	65.0 percent
Providing care for the pet outside school hours	49.3 percent
Managing students' interactions with the pet (for example, being gentle and taking turns)	16.9 percent
Having the pet distract the students from their schoolwork	14.3 percent
Managing health issues of the pet	12.1 percent
Integrating the pet into lessons, while still meeting teaching requirements	10.0 percent
Managing student and animal safety issues	8.2 percent
Learning how to take care of this type of pet	7.9 percent
Managing any student allergy issues	5.9 percent
Getting permission for my school to have a classroom pet	4.5 percent
Getting permission from the students' parents to have a classroom pet	1.1 percent
None of the preceding	12.4 percent
Other (please specify)	5.5 percent

Source: Adapted from American Humane Association, 2015, p. 28. Used with permission.

Figure 2.1: Challenges to classroom pets.

- Student interactions with the classroom animal
- Liability and safety issues
- Health concerns
- Cultural issues
- Teacher work overload

Cost

As you might expect, having an animal in the classroom can incur additional costs for a teacher already on an extremely tight budget. The solution to this obstacle can be as easy as you, the teacher, just dipping into your own pocket for those extra dollars—but this doesn't seem quite fair. Fear not—there are ways to come up with the needed funds for purchasing not just the animal but also everything else involved in having animals in your classroom.

Applying for a grant is the most logical and straightforward approach to this funding problem. However, if you are like me—someone who has applied for grants before—you are probably rolling your eyes because you are well aware of the potential time-consuming process nightmare, one for which there is no guaranteed payoff for a lot of time, energy, and effort on your part. Rest assured, because there is a fantastic educational grant program called *Pets in the Classroom* (see https://petsintheclassroom.org/grant-app). The Pet Care Trust established this program to help teachers acquire funding for animals and related supplies. Through the Pet Care Trust grant process, you can obtain funds for the purchase of new animals, their environments, food, and even supplies for existing classroom animals, all through a direct, no-hassle online application. I simply cannot say enough great things about the folks at Pet Care Trust and their supporting organizations (World Pet Association [https://worldpetassociation.org], Pet Industry Distributors Association [https://pida.org], and American Pet Products Association [https://americanpetproducts.org]). They recognize the benefits of animals in the classroom and, more important, also recognize many teachers may have limited resources.

As of 2014, the Pets in the Classroom project has provided over 50,000 teachers with animals and supplies, which directly affected the lives of around 2.5 million students. The best news is this application process is very quick and easy and doesn't involve keeping your fingers crossed, hoping you might get accepted. *If you qualify, you will receive grant money.* The qualification process involves three simple questions to confirm your eligibility. Check out https://petsintheclassroom.org/grant-app to start your application.

> "I say go for it; it is definitely possible and realistic for teachers to get a grant. Last year, I got a $1,600 grant from the Arizona Diamondbacks professional baseball team, of all places, and was able to buy a python, supplies, and food. The students simply love it."
>
> —**CALE MORRIS,** *middle school teacher, Arizona*
> *(personal communication, April 4, 2018)*

Another potential funding source could be your state's Department of Natural Resources (DNR). Each state often has grant programs that make funds available for educators dealing with local flora and fauna of special interest. In my home state of Maryland, the DNR has projects that provide classrooms with a wide selection of organisms, including terrapins, horseshoe crabs, trout, sea grasses, and other target species related to the health of the Chesapeake Bay. The DNR provides not only the animal but also the setup, an enclosure, technical assistance, and expert guidance. This particular project—again a head-start program—revolves around students raising the animals over the course of the school year and then releasing them into the wild at the end of the school year. This is an excellent way for educators to get animals in the classroom, and it also allows students to gain an appreciation for the target species, lets the DNR raise awareness of the species and local environments, and benefits the local ecosystem. That's just good for everyone. Further, these DNR head-start programs usually generate positive press coverage (on local television and radio, and in print), which is something school administrators always enjoy. A story involving local students, educators, and an endangered species is usually highly sought-after by the media. This kind of feel-good press coverage is a powerful tool that helps change the attitudes and opinions of principals, school board members, and superintendents when it comes to animals in the classroom.

Yet another great way to help defray some of the cost of having animals in the classroom is to contact local university biology departments, nearby research labs, and even zoos, aquariums, and wildlife centers. In my experience, these types of organizations sometimes have old aquariums, supplies, and cages they are more than happy to donate to schools. When I was a part of the University of Miami in 1996, we had piles of such supplies in the basement, and the faculty was just looking for ways to purge some of the excess. This is a great way to get a lot of what you need at little or no cost. I've even had success contacting companies that produce aquariums, reptile supplies, enclosures, and other animal care products directly. Many of these businesses will make imperfect or damaged products available to educators at no cost.

Middle school teacher Cale Morris says he knew purchasing a classroom animal might be expensive, but he was surprised at the cost for maintaining the animal. Here, he explains how to defray those costs:

> I initiated a program where students can receive extra credit if they bring in a frozen rat for the class snake to eat. These students are also rewarded with extra time interacting with the snake, or other such incentives. This dramatically brings down the cost of buying frozen rats, which can be expensive. In addition, I visited numerous pet stores and asked for class discounts. Two stores agreed to grant me a 10 percent discount on anything purchased by me or my students that was for our classroom animals. You could do the same thing for other types of animals—everything from feeder guppies to hamster food. The kids just love being involved in this capacity, giving them a special connection to the animal. (C. Morris, personal communication, April 4, 2018)

As Cale mentions, one ongoing cost is food for your classroom animal. He chose to minimize this cost by having students bring in food for the classroom animal to eat, but depending on the animal you select, food can actually be quite inexpensive, especially if you choose to start a colony of fruit flies or mealworms. Many small classroom animals eat tiny prey like fruit flies, including small lizards, frogs, toads, spiders, and even insects like praying mantises. Mealworms are a great food source for frogs, toads, lizards, birds, salamanders, scorpions, tarantulas, and many others. Creating a self-sustaining food colony is a great idea to minimize food costs—and it serves the additional benefit of bringing even more animals (or insects) into your classroom. Appendix B (page 99) contains helpful guides on how you and your students can start a self-sustaining colony of mealworms or fruit flies.

Daily Animal Care

Animal care is without a doubt the most important undertaking in the entire animals-in-the-classroom process. The living creatures under your care rely on you and your students to provide them with everything they need to survive. They deserve proper care and maintenance in return for what they provide you and your students. With animal ownership comes great responsibility, so you must prepare for the daily responsibilities of animal care before you bring one into your classroom.

First, the creatures under your care will require at the very least a daily inspection. Do your research when deciding which animal is right for your classroom because some animals will require more time than others. Mammals and birds are notorious for requiring more attention than, say, a snake or an ant farm, where a cursory inspection is all that might be needed. Those animals with a slow metabolism, the *ectotherms* (reptiles and amphibians), may not require daily feeding and cleaning. Snakes, for example, only eat and drink every few weeks. As a result, snakes do not defecate on a daily basis, and thus daily cleanup and maintenance for snakes is minimal. You may find yourself simply needing to make sure the cage is secure, the animal is alive and well, and clean water is present—tasks students can complete in under a minute! For these reasons, this type of classroom animal is popular with teachers.

However, most classroom animals will require a bit more attention. Fall into the habit of practicing what I call *IFWC* on a daily basis—that is, *inspect, feed, water,* and *clean*. Regardless of the animal, you, as the teacher, should complete every one of these checks when you first enter your classroom each day. A quick inspection will suffice—simply make sure the animal is actually where it's supposed to be (in the enclosure), it is alive (letting students discover a dead animal can be bad), its enclosure is secure, and all features (lights, heaters, misters, and so on) are operational.

Regardless of whether the animal eats on a daily basis, you should look for and remove any old food in the enclosure. I have found that many animal odor problems do not come from the animal, but rather from old and rotting food left inside the enclosure. Leaving old food laying around can result in mold, mildew, fruit flies, maggots, or worse. A clean animal enclosure not only helps keep your animal healthy but also you and your students. In addition, inspecting and removing uneaten food on a daily basis allows you to monitor your animal's health and well-being. It's also a great idea to keep records—you can nominate a student to be in charge of this—and monitor how much the animal is eating. Many times when food goes uneaten, it can be an early indicator of a sick animal.

Providing clean, fresh water for your classroom animal is the most important thing you must provide on a daily basis. Animals can live a lot longer without food than they can without water, so *always* make sure water is readily available for your classroom critter. It's even a good idea to check on its water at the beginning and the end of each day.

Keeping your animal's enclosure clean is an obvious part of animal care. This is a good activity for students to undertake before classes begin. I always had students arrive early (before school started) to do enclosure cleaning. That way, you don't have dung-creating foul odors in the classroom all day. Most enclosure cleaning is quick and simple. To begin, remove the newspapers, sand, and wood chips (or whatever the animal requires) lining the bottom of the cage. Then, give the enclosure a quick clean with soap and water, vinegar solution, or another suitable disinfectant; add a new substrate; and you're done! Always make sure you have plenty of old newspapers (or other substrate materials) on hand. Nothing is more frustrating than getting the tank nice and clean only to then find you are out of wood chips or newspapers!

At first, following the IFWC steps for each of your animals might seem a little time consuming, but with practice and a daily routine, the process will become quick and easy. Remember, your most valuable resource in all of this is your extra hands—your students. They can—and should—play an important and vital role in cleaning and maintaining your classroom animals. Ideally, at some point you should just fall into a supervisory role, letting the students manage the animals on a daily basis. Just remember IFWC!

Tales From the Front Lines
Turtle Juice

A teacher from northern Illinois, Mrs. M., shared a story with me involving how *not* to empty a turtle tank. Her classroom featured a large aquarium filled with all sorts of aquatic turtles. It was a real thing of beauty, set up to look like a natural turtle habitat. It was the envy of other classes and seemed to be the hit of every Back to School Night when parents were instructed they *must* go see the turtle tank.

Since the turtle tank was so popular and such a source of pride and joy for so many, Mrs. M. always made sure it was clean and in pristine condition. This involved weekly water changes, which meant removing about a third of the water and replacing it with new fresh water. Normally, the students used small buckets to remove the desired amount of water, carried them across the room and out the door, and emptied them outside, a process that usually left a trail of water from sloshing buckets across the room.

One particular weekend, Mrs. M. decided the tank needed a water change. Without any students around and being short on time, she realized she would have to do the work herself. She decided that instead of making many trips across the room with buckets, she was going to let gravity do the work. She figured by using a hose and siphoning the water out of the tank, she could get the job done in half the time, allowing her to get back to her weekend. She stretched

>>

the hose from the tank across the room and out the door, where it would empty.

Siphoning relies on gravity to move a liquid through a hose. To get the water to start flowing, you must remove the air from inside the hose. To do that, Mrs. M. used her mouth, sucking on the end of the hose to get the water moving. Her plan (as is typical of anyone who has siphoned before) was to remove her mouth from the end of the hose right before she got a mouthful of turtle water. In theory this was a great plan; however, Mrs. M. miscalculated how fast the water was moving through her hose, and she suddenly got an unexpected surprise—a mouth full of fetid turtle tank water.

She immediately spit out the turtle water. Although embarrassed and slightly revolted, she was no worse for wear. The tank emptied quickly, and she got the water changed without further incident. She was then free to enjoy the rest of her weekend . . . or so she thought. Later, Mrs. M. started getting stomach cramps and a headache; she began feeling pretty awful. It turned out the turtle tank water in her mouth was coming back to haunt her. She contracted a salmonella infection from the turtle water and spent a few days feeling under the weather.

There is an important lesson here for all of us. No matter how clean you think your classroom animals are, there are always unseen dangers, like bacteria! That is why hand washing with soap and water and a strict cleaning protocol are vitally important when you have animals in the classroom. Finally, do not under any circumstance siphon water out of an aquarium with your mouth, no matter how fast you think you are! You just might get an unexpected mouthful of turtle juice . . . and a few unexpected days off!

Figure 2.2 is a data sheet you can use for tracking the daily care of your classroom animals.

Animal Care During School Breaks

In the AHA (2015) study involving 1,200 teachers, the second most frequently cited obstacle to having animals in the classroom is caring for the animals during school breaks. This is an obstacle easy to overcome if you just exercise reasonable judgement.

Animal Data Sheet

Common Name:				Cage Number:		
Scientific Name:				Food Type:		
Given Name:				Date Acquired:		

Date	Weight	Length	Food	Cage Cleaned	Notes *(for example, skin shed, amount of food eaten)*

Figure 2.2: Classroom animal care data sheet.

Visit go.SolutionTree.com/instruction for a free reproducible version of this figure.

The solution can be as easy as finding someone who will be in the building during breaks. When I was a teacher, my department head would come into the school at some point every single day, 365 days a year, no exceptions. This made it easy for me because he was happy to look in on my animals and make sure the power was on and everything was operating. If you know of someone who is going to be in the building each day (such as a principal, an administrator, or a caretaker), you could consider asking him or her to care for your animals during breaks.

If a person is not available to check on your animals, see what automatic technologies you can find that may be appropriate. In some instances, the lights, heaters, and water misters in your animal's enclosure can (and should) be kept on electrical timers, making daily attendance unnecessary. Adequate water and food for those that need it (like guinea pigs, rats, tortoises, and hermit crabs) are many times simply placed in the enclosures or dispensed by a mechanical feeder, which can cover the animal's care over the course of a long weekend. Mechanical feeders for aquariums that dispense the proper amount of food daily is a fantastic way to get your animals through even extended breaks.

However, some animals do need daily attention and for those, care during breaks gets a little more complicated. One of the ways I found to be really successful when I was teaching was to let students bring their own pets into the classroom. I had one student who was just crazy about animals, and he had a virtual menagerie at home. Early in the school year, he offered to bring in a few of his animals to live in our classroom—or *loaner animals*, if you will. The animals still belonged to this student, but the class got to maintain them. It was a great situation because the class got the benefit of having animals in the classroom, and the student got the benefit of ownership—and most important, he would take the animals home with him during school breaks, solving the problem of providing care during breaks. Additionally, the student got a lot of pride and satisfaction from being the resident expert on the animals, and also from the rest of the students knowing the animals were his. That was his thing. He wasn't an athlete or a musician, and he wasn't into drama or school clubs. Instead, he was the "animal guy," and he relished it! I would be surprised if every school didn't have an animal girl or guy who could help you out in this manner, thus solving the school breaks–care hurdle.

However, sometimes you just cannot get around the obstacle of animal care during breaks, meaning the job falls on you or a trusted student you select. Many teachers have told me they have had wonderful results by having students take home the class guinea pig or lizard during school breaks. Oftentimes, schools have an after-school club (such as the Green Team or Nature Nuts) centered on nature and conservation. These clubs normally have a number of dedicated, reliable students you could choose from. At my children's elementary school, teachers utilize Green Team club members. The teachers make "vacation animal care" a reward for the students who work the hardest and show the most responsible behavior. Again, the bottom line here is for you to use reasonable judgement and precautions when selecting the right student for these tasks. It is a good idea, and common sense, to get parental permission before sending home any animal with a student. Requiring a signed parental permission slip is a good approach because then you have consent in writing and avoid any miscommunication. You probably don't want a phone call from a parent on the Friday night of a long school weekend asking why his or her child came home with the classroom gerbil!

A teacher once told me he tries to make animal care during breaks as easy and foolproof as possible. His plan involves using a big, clear plastic bin for each animal going home with a student during breaks; these bins include everything needed for the animals' care. Each bin has laminated instructions attached to the lid listing all care and feeding directions. The list is clear, easy to understand, and well defined, eliminating any ambiguity or questions. It includes a numbered checklist so the student can document when everything is completed daily. This teacher also told me the parents of the student taking home an animal come in during the last day of school to go over all the specifics, so the student and his or her parents know exactly what to expect. I think this is an outstanding way to deal with animal care over breaks.

Lastly, sometimes businesses will assist in animal babysitting during breaks. My learning center, Eco Adventures (https://ecoadventures.org), is one such business, and others in the United States include Avian and Exotic Pet Care (www.avianpetcare.com), Pet Sitters (www.petsitter.com), and Bat Country Pet Sitting (www.batcopetsitting.com). Regardless of how you approach holiday animal care, you must ensure all classroom animals have adequate food and water, light and heat (when applicable), and clean living spaces—even when school is not open.

Student Interactions With the Classroom Animal

Managing student interactions with classroom animals is an important part of their care, and you simply cannot get complacent about this. When I was teaching, I had a very strict protocol for any animal interactions, and you should too. In my opinion, this is the single most important part of having animals in the classroom. Correct animal interaction management helps avoid problems, especially injury to animals and students. Many animals can be delicate to touch (like frogs with their sensitive skin), whereas others can cause harm to students (like biting lizards or snakes). Again, managing appropriate student-animal interactions comes down to common sense and using reasonable precautions and judgement.

While there are specific rules of engagement for each animal (and I list a few here and more in appendix A, page 95), I won't list them all because there are simply just too many. All you really need to do is your homework on the personalities, behaviors, and abilities of your classroom animals. Following is a list of a few examples of animal-interaction rules I used in my classroom. These rules are standard procedure (and common sense) when students and animals interact.

- We show respect for the animal at all times; no crowding, pushing, shoving, panicking, screaming, or unauthorized touching allowed.
- We always practice a *two-finger touch*, with the index and middle finger extended. This prevents students from squeezing, poking, annoying, hurting, or stressing out the animal.
- When it comes to snakes or other critters that could bite, students are only allowed to touch the animal near the middle of its body. Even with super-friendly, trusted snakes, this must be standard procedure to avoid potential bites.
- When it comes to frogs or salamanders, students must moisten their fingers with water before touching because these animals have very thin, sensitive skin.
- Most important, I strictly enforce hand washing with soap and water after touching any animal to avoid diseases such as salmonella.

These rules are all common sense. Use reasonable judgement and take reasonable precautions to come up with well-defined rules and then enforce them.

While there are general rules that apply to all animals (such as those previously listed), there are also more specific rules that apply to certain animals. Following are a few examples.

Snakes

Whenever presenting a snake for interaction, always hold it using the *wine bottle hold*—that is, like a waiter presenting a bottle of wine to a table. Hold your hands out in front of you with your lower hand supporting the snake's body (the bottom of the wine bottle) and the upper hand controlling the head (the neck of the wine bottle). This way, students can safely touch the body while the head (the potentially biting end) is safely controlled, away from all interaction.

Always keep the head of the snake away from students. Be sure students always touch using just two fingers and never around the snake's head or tail. While touching, only run fingers in the head-to-tail direction—the direction the scales run—to prevent irritating the snake.

Hedgehogs

Be careful of the *spines* (the hollow hairs or quills made stiff with keratin), which is the potential problem element of this animal. Handling a hedgehog is kind of like holding a pin cushion—it can be tricky, and it must be done very gingerly! I always use a towel over my cupped hands, making a bowl to cradle the hedgehog. This prevents the holder from getting spiked, plus the towel adds a layer of protection against defecation. Hedgehogs are notorious poopers! As with snakes, only use the two-finger touch, and only run fingers in the head-to-tail direction to prevent being spiked. The spines lay down in that direction when hedgehogs relax and are brought upright for protection. Also avoid touching the hedgehog's head; wild animals do not like being touched on the head.

Tarantulas

Cupped hands are vital when picking up as well as holding tarantulas. If a tarantula happens to be in a biting mood, your cupped hands prevent its fangs from reaching your skin. When your hands are flat, they form a flat surface, and the tarantula's fangs can bite you . . . so heed this warning. When picking up a tarantula, bring your cupped hands in from the sides of the spider (where the legs are). As you slowly bring your hands together, the spider should move its legs up onto your hands.

While holding the spider, it is important to hold it close to the floor or over a table or podium—something that will prevent the spider from falling a great distance if dropped. Tarantulas are very delicate, and a fall from any height will result in their death. While holding spiders, try to avoid any sudden movements because they are extremely sensitive animals and respond to even minute movements of air. If the spider starts to walk while you are holding it, simply move your hand one over the next like a treadmill, thus allowing the spider to walk in place. *Never* hold the spider close to anyone's face because the spider can flick small hairs (*urticating hairs*) off its abdomen that are very irritating to human eyes and skin. This is one of the spider's defense mechanisms. *Never* touch the abdomen, or you are simply asking to get urticated!

Finally, always be on the lookout for signals that the spider is stressed. It will let you know. If it raises its *pedipalps* (short, front-stroking appendages) into the air, it is unhappy. Oftentimes, along with the raising of the pedipalps, the tarantula will erect its fangs—a pretty obvious sign the spider has had enough handling. Also, if the spider's back legs start stroking its abdomen, that is a sign the spider is dislodging the urticating hairs into the air. If this happens, it's best to put the spider down. Tarantulas can be fantastic animals for the classroom; they just need more attention to detail than many other critters.

Liability and Safety Issues

Liability and safety issues are big hurdles, maybe the biggest. Liability lawsuits are frequently the deal-breakers for having animals in the classroom. My daughter's middle school simply does not allow animals in the school—period. No questions asked, no debate, no exceptions. Nothing has ever happened to prompt such a policy (there was never an incident between a student and an animal, for example). It was simply a case of someone sometime just deciding this is the policy. I have tried many times to get an exception—for example, to take animals into her school for a presentation—but have found it is impossible. There is no explanation or rationale for such a policy. Sadly, the losers here are the students.

Many school districts say their insurance policy does not cover classroom animals. In our litigious society, schools have been sued for classroom animal incidents (Fisicaro, 2017). School superintendents must make some tough decisions. If you teach in a school with strict policies about classroom animals, you may find yourself in a difficult uphill battle, though it's definitely a battle worth fighting. Try getting members of your school board and Parent-Teacher Association (PTA) involved because having them on board with your cause can really help. You will need to educate them as much as possible with supportive materials. You might try some of the following ideas.

- Get testimonials from teachers in other school districts.
- Ask your students and parents to write letters of support.
- Organize local animal experts to give informational lectures and be available for in-depth question-and-answer sessions.
- Invite local health officials supportive of your cause to speak at meetings.
- Bring animals to an association meeting for an educational meet and greet.

Anything along these lines can help convince your potential allies (like PTA and school board members) of the importance of animals in the classroom. There are even situations where parents, students, and educators are starting to fight back against overly restrictive policies by starting petitions and organizing rallies (Fisicaro, 2017; Kendrick, 2016). Change is always possible, and a lot of these policies were enacted on false information or misconceptions—like the myth that all reptiles are infected with salmonella. Educating those in power at the district level can yield change. Making a reasonable, well-thought-out case using the many studies supporting the benefits of animals in the classroom can be a powerful argument.

Ultimately, the best way to prevent against accidents in the classroom is to religiously follow the guidelines laid out in this book and other care instruction manuals relating to your classroom animal. Always use reasonable judgment and common sense, as you and your students already do with all other classroom rules, and you should not have any problems.

> "My school doesn't have a written policy on animals in the classroom, but they do support them. My principal, superintendent, and school board all agree that our animals have made a difference in the lives of our students at all levels. Some local schools that have had a strict no-animal policy have actually changed their position on them after they have seen the impact that animals had on our students."
>
> —**PAUL RITTER,** *high school ecology teacher, Illinois*
> *(personal communication, February 16, 2018)*

Health Concerns

Many students have allergies; therefore, as an educator, you simply must take this into consideration when deciding on a classroom animal. Animals with hair or feathers are the usual culprits, but many times this doesn't have to be a deal-breaker. I have seen many classrooms with mammals even when some students are allergic. These classrooms simply employ a strategy where the animals are kept in a specific part of the room, as far away from the allergic students as possible. In addition, teachers don't allow the allergic students to closely interact with those animals. I am told this can be an effective strategy. The easier approach is to avoid mammals and birds if you know of students with specific, acute allergies to these types of animals, making it essential for you to identify these students as soon as possible.

The other major health concern I previously touched on is hygiene. Germs, bacteria, viruses, and grime are part of the deal when associating with animals. Salmonella is the one that seems to be most frequently brought up when it comes to animals in the classroom. *Salmonella* is a common bacterium found in the digestive tracts of animals—humans included—and it also turns up on lots of foods. People are usually infected orally, and salmonella is one of the most common causes of food poisoning. You can avoid salmonella using reasonable precautions, like hand washing. Therefore, it is absolutely essential to adhere to a strict soap-and-water hand-washing policy when interacting with any animal. I see hand sanitizer in virtually every classroom I visit, and that stuff is a good addition, but not nearly as effective as good old soap-and-water hand washing. Figure 2.3 provides further hand-washing tips the Centers for Disease Control and Prevention (CDC; n.d.b) recommends; you can print out and post these tips above your hand-washing station. In addition, a solution of water and white vinegar (to spray down surfaces) is also an extremely effective way to keep those pesky germs at bay. As always, simply use common sense, good hygienic practices, and reasonable precautions and judgment (for example, no hands in mouth), and you and your students will be fine.

---

1. Wet your hands with running water, then turn off the tap to avoid wasting water.
2. Lather your hands by rubbing them together with soap.
3. Be sure to lather the backs of your hands, between your fingers, and under your nails. (Wash hands for twenty seconds or sing "Happy Birthday" twice.)
4. Rinse your hands well under clean, running water.
5. Dry with clean towel or air dry.

BE SURE TO . . .
- Wash your hands before and after handling a pet.
- Wash your hands before and after handling pet supplies and equipment.
- Wash your hands before and after cleaning your pet's habitat.

Source: Adapted from Centers for Disease Control and Prevention, n.d.b.

Figure 2.3: Rules for pet care hand washing.

Visit go.SolutionTree.com/instruction for a free reproducible version of this figure.

Cultural Issues

A teacher in Arizona conveyed a story to me about an incident in his classroom that deserves mentioning. This particular teacher had snakes in his classroom, and a conflict arose with a Native American student. The student's tribe believes it is taboo

> ### Tales From the Front Lines
> ## Your New Best Friend... Soap!
>
> If you don't already have a close relationship with soap, you need to find one if you want to keep animals in your classroom. It will definitely become your new best friend. You should thank your lucky stars each and every time you and your students lather up. This amazing substance isn't some newfound miracle that helps keep us safe from smudges and stains; in fact, it's been around for thousands of years. Researchers discovered evidence of soap during excavations of ancient Babylonia, tracing its history back to 2800 BC (Soap History, n.d.). Our good buddy soap has marched through the ages doing what it does best: getting stuff clean. Egyptians were crazy about bathing with soap. Romans loved it. Greeks swore by its cleansing abilities, and through the ages, British royalty couldn't get enough of it (Ross, 2016). Few things persist for thousands of years, but soap did, and the reason why is that it's superb at what it does—*clean*.
>
> This brings up the excellent question, Exactly how does soap get things so clean? Soap molecules are made up of two dramatically different ends. One end of the molecule loves water—that's called *hydrophilic*—whereas the other end hates the stuff—that's called *hydrophobic*. The hydrophobic end actually loves oils and grease, so it's also called *lipophilic*. The lipophilic end of the soap molecule is where all the action takes place because it attaches itself to grime, grease, bacteria, and oils. Once attached, it hangs on tight. All the while, the other end of the soap molecule, the hydrophilic end, just follows the water because it loves water. So where the water goes, so does the soap molecule, with the attached grime on its opposite end. Where does it go? It follows the water right down the drain when you are washing your hands (immediately after you have handled your classroom turtle, right?).
>
> Soap is amazing stuff! Plain old water just doesn't have cleaning properties, so it isn't going to keep you and your students safe. And don't be fooled by the high-tech hand sanitizers that are all the rage, many of them touting 100 percent effectiveness against all germs (note: defining a germ is tricky). Hand sanitizers are simply not as effective as good old soap-and-water hand washing (Centers for Disease Control and Prevention, n.d.c.). There is a reason why surgeons wash their hands the old-fashioned way—with soap and water—before operating on a patient. There is simply no substitute for our good buddy, soap. If it's not already, make soap your new best friend when inviting animals into your classroom!

to be in the same room with snakes, and therefore the tribal elders asked the school principal to remove the snakes. This is a great example of how unanticipated cultural or religious beliefs may conflict with the presence of animals in your classroom.

Some cultures believe particular animals are unclean so people need to avoid them, whereas other religions actually revere particular animals and associate them with gods. Teachers must practice cultural sensitivity at all times, so it is important to identify potential issues early on to ensure your animals are all culturally appropriate. A questionnaire sent home with students for their parents at the beginning of the school year is the perfect way to identify any potential problems.

Teacher Work Overload

Many teachers I speak with say their workload can be simply overwhelming, and there just isn't time to pursue having animals in their classrooms. On this issue, they are preaching to the choir because I have been there and experienced it. Granted, animals in the classroom take up some extra time initially, but once established, the benefits you and your class will experience far outweigh the minimal time expenditure for maintaining them.

One teacher summed up his feelings about the added commitment of classroom animals and whether it is worth it. He told me his students just "go crazy" for the animals, and he uses the animals as incentives for students to exhibit good behavior. He says, "It's true that having animals requires more work, but my job is much easier in the long run because my students are motivated to behave themselves, and I have fewer discipline problems than teachers without animals, thus making my job easier" (C. Morris, personal communication, April 6, 2018).

Help yourself by utilizing student helpers, assistants, or caretakers. You will be doing these students a favor when you allow them to take part in the care and maintenance of classroom animals. When I was a high school teacher, at times my workload seemed unmanageable. Most problematic was I taught four different subjects in four different rooms in four different parts of the building—yikes! I had a big, old cart I would load up with all my teaching gear and roll around the hallways when switching classrooms. This situation—or any situation where a teacher may have to move between classrooms with regularity—can make having animals in the classroom challenging, but it is by no means impossible. The teachers with whom I shared classrooms were supportive of having animals in the classroom, which was critical. Having these other teachers involved and on board with the animals made for a manageable situation. At the beginning of the year, the teachers had a group meeting and laid out the rules and regulations surrounding the animals. In practice, the animals were actually really beneficial for all. The other teachers' classes got to benefit from the animals, as did mine, which would not have occurred (or would have been more difficult) if we all had our own classrooms. Sharing classrooms also divided the labor between different teachers and students, making the demands of animal care less daunting. It's important for all teachers involved to agree to and adhere to the same animal handling procedures and protocol. This is vital for the animals' and students' well-being. You too can push a loaded-down cart around the school to different classrooms and still enjoy the benefits of animals in the classroom.

Conclusion

This chapter outlined several hurdles to animals in the classroom, including cost, daily care, health concerns, and cultural issues. It would be easy to look at all of these obstacles and think that these are too many things to deal with when you are already faced with lesson planning, grading, and parent-teacher conferences. It's true that having animals in your classroom is a lot like having children: there is definitely a lot involved in keeping them safe, happy, and healthy, but the benefits far outweigh the time and energy spent maintaining them. The aim of this chapter was not to overwhelm you but merely to point out the elements you need to consider and responsibly deal with. Simply following the guidelines outlined in this chapter will minimize headaches, streamline the process, and ensure that you have confidence in your classroom animal and all that it entails.

Once you are confident that you can handle the hurdles, you are ready to take the leap and choose the perfect animal for you and your students! An easy approach to animal selection is the topic of the next chapter.

Cross-Curricular Lesson Ideas

Mathematics and Technology

"American Humane is committed to ensuring the safety, welfare and well-being of all animals" (American Humane Association [AHA], n.d.). Students can research the AHA website (https://americanhumane.org) to learn more. Using information they collect, students can create an infographic to present a data story about AHA and what it does. Students may choose to include a call to action in supporting AHA's work.

Music

There is nothing better than a catchy tune to help students remember important information. Using steps from the hand-washing chart, along with information about the history of soap (see page 43), have students create a hand-washing song. Students should include a verse and chorus with a catchy melody.

Reading, Social Studies, and Social and Emotional Learning (SEL)

Native American storytelling has a very rich history. Different tribes have varying stories, but most are founded in common lessons or themes that often include animals. Traditions, customs, and legends once shared only through oral traditions can now be found in many children's books. For younger learners, you may want to check out books from your library or create a classroom library that includes Joseph and James Bruchac's books, such as *How the Chipmunk Got Its Stripes* and *Turtle's Race With Beaver*. These stories support SEL because the characters focus on solving conflicts and showing humility, anger, pride, and support for one another. Older students may choose to study Native American symbols and their meanings.

Mathematics and English Language Arts

Students can research organizations that offer classroom grants to create a graph depicting the funding amounts. They may also want to include other data, such as how often funding takes place or how many grants are offered. This can help students understand the process and requirements that must be met when applying for grant funding while providing information about possible funding sources.

Younger students may choose to write a letter to an organization, family members, or friends persuading them to donate funds for a classroom animal.

CHAPTER 3
How to Select the Perfect Animal

Once you have the all-clear to introduce an animal to your classroom, you are at the fun stage of the journey—selecting the perfect animal! Although this step may be exciting for both you and your students, it is still important to take your time in selecting your classroom animal. Just because the offer of a free parrot looks and sounds great, you don't want to find yourself in a difficult, desperate, and unprepared situation, so take it slow and do your research. No animal should ever be brought into the classroom without a lot of thought and planning.

The National Science Teaching Association's (NSTA, 2008) position statement, *Responsible Use of Live Animals and Dissection in the Science Classroom*, recommends when selecting an animal, teachers should:

- Educate themselves about the safe and responsible use of animals in the classroom. Teachers should seek information from reputable sources and familiarize themselves with laws and regulations in their state.
- Become knowledgeable about the acquisition and care of animals appropriate to the species under study so that both students and the animals stay safe and healthy during all activities.
- Follow local, state, and national laws, policies, and regulations when live organisms, particularly native species, are included in the classroom.

You must determine what is even possible in your school and state (abide by regulations) to determine which animal will be most suitable for your classroom. When it comes to rules and regulations involving animals in the classroom, each state—and even different parts of each state—may have policies involving animals. Check your state's specific regulations because you definitely don't want to be involved in an embarrassing situation with the long arm of the law! A great place to find this information is your state's Department of Natural Resources website. In addition, the NABT (n.d.) has a comprehensive list; I highly recommend checking this resource to see if it includes your state's guidelines.

After following these guidelines and checking the rules and regulations pertaining to your school and state, you should consider the following factors when selecting your classroom animal.

- Student preferences
- Allergies
- Age appropriateness
- Life span
- Need for care during school breaks
- Available space
- Endangered status

This chapter will help you navigate each of these issues as you make the big decision regarding which animal (or animals) is right for your classroom and students.

Student Preferences

Another big decision you must make is whether to include your students in choosing the animal for the classroom. Allowing students to participate and have a voice in the selection is a great way for them to feel ownership of the animal. In my experience, by involving students in the selection process, they show much more dedication and passion toward the classroom animal than those students in situations where a new animal just shows up one day. Including your students will make them feel a connection to the animal, which is always important. Allowing students to name a classroom animal can also generate strong feelings toward the new addition.

It can be a lot of fun letting your students help select the animal—within reason, of course—as some will suggest a rattlesnake or Gila monster. Use the selection process as a great learning situation by involving your students. Discuss why some animals won't make good classroom additions (such as spitting cobras) and why others will (such as hamsters). Go over the pros and cons of potential candidates, have students research the animal options, discuss the space and other requirements of each candidate, and then debate or even vote for the winning selection. At the end of the day, however, the animal decision will lay on your shoulders, so choose wisely.

Allergies

As mentioned in chapter 2 (page 27), it is important to remember not all students can interact with just any animal. Sending home a questionnaire for parents is a great first step in identifying children with allergies. In this same questionnaire, you might also want to identify any cultural problems with potential animals (see Cultural Issues, page 42). Further, it's not only the students you need to consider when thinking about allergies but also other teachers, staff, and building employees. After you've already acquired your classroom parrot, you don't want to find out the custodian is severely allergic to feathers. You might end up having to mop your own classroom floor! If you do discover students or staff with allergy issues, there are easy alternatives. Since fur and feathers are the usual culprits when it comes to allergic reactions, reptiles, amphibians, insects, and fish are great candidates.

Figure 3.1 (page 52) provides a sample questionnaire for parents to complete before you bring animals into your classroom. You can easily adapt the questions here for staff as well.

> "I was told so many problem stories about allergies, angry parents, mess and smell, huge allocations of time and money, bites, scratches, injuries . . . the list just goes on and on. But I have found my classroom animals create none of these problems. They have been nothing short of pure pleasure for all who interact with them, and have been quite easy to maintain. All the stories I heard were just that—stories!"
>
> —**JERRY JOHNSTON**, *sixth-grade biology teacher, Florida*
> *(personal communication, May 15, 2019)*

Age Appropriateness

Age appropriateness is another element to consider before selecting your classroom animal. Letting first-graders handle a tarantula probably isn't the best decision. Animals requiring minimal care or expertise—and that aren't known biters—are best for K–3 students. Hermit crabs, aquarium fish, gerbils, toads, and even ant farms are all great candidates for younger students. Turtles and tortoises also make great classroom animals for this age group, as long as you remember to follow a strict hygiene protocol and don't allow any hands in mouths!

Parent Name: _____

Student Name: _____

Date: _____

We will be holding and interacting with a variety of live animals in science class this year. Most of the animals students will be interacting with are snakes, lizards, tortoises, rabbits, hedgehogs, and millipedes. These animals are safe for students to handle. Students will also be viewing, but not holding, some venomous animals like tarantulas and scorpions. Please complete this questionnaire to help me better understand the needs of your child.

1. Has your child ever had allergic reactions to mammals or birds? (Circle one.)

    YES   NO

    If yes, please list the names of the animals:

    _____

2. Has your child ever had an allergic reaction to insects or other types of bugs? (Circle one.)

    YES   NO

    If yes, please list the names of the bugs:

    _____

3. Do you have any other concerns about your child being around animals? Please describe.

    _____
    _____
    _____

If you have any questions or concerns, please email me anytime.

Thank you.

Figure 3.1: Animals in the classroom allergy questionnaire for parents.

*Visit **go.SolutionTree.com/instruction** for a free reproducible version of this figure.*

Life Span

Nothing lives forever, including classroom animals, so life span is another thing to consider when selecting your classroom animal. Be forewarned: with some animals, you will definitely be in it for the long haul. Certain birds and tortoises can outlive you, with life spans approaching one hundred years. Unless you plan on teaching for the next several decades (or plan on taking the animal with you when you retire), box turtles and parrots probably shouldn't be among your choices. On the flip side, death is inevitable and can be a downer, but dealing with the death of a classroom animal can also be a powerful teaching tool and life lesson. The death of a classroom animal can introduce students to the concept of death and help them deal with situations when they arise within their own families or the community. "The loss of a classroom pet allows students to explore the intimidating concept of death by examining how society handles grief as well as the emotions and repercussions of this inevitable life process" (Pets in the Classroom, n.d.). The Pets in the Classroom website (www.petsintheclassroom.org) has a great resource page for teachers on how to handle the death of a classroom animal, discussing factors such as terminology, the need for appropriate conversations, and how to notify families.

Here are a few average life spans of potential classroom animals.

- Praying mantis, garden spider—six months to a year
- Leopard frog, rabbit, mouse—two years
- Gerbil—four years
- Guinea pig, corn snake, leopard gecko—seven years
- Finch—eight years
- Goldfish, parakeet, bearded dragon, common toad, tarantula—ten years
- Hermit crab—twenty years
- Box turtle—fifty years
- Cockatoo—seventy years

Tales From the Front Lines

Show-and-Tell Surprise!

Mrs. C., a teacher in Indiana, shared a great story with me concerning a show-and-tell object. One of her students brought in a small "cocoon" she found on her family Christmas tree. Her family had cut down a live tree, and while they were decorating it, she found the interesting little "cocoon." She snipped off the twig it was attached to and brought it to her class to share with the other students. She wasn't quite sure what was inside, but she found it fun to marvel at what it might be. The class was full of ideas. Was it a beautiful butterfly or maybe a giant moth? They all wanted to know for sure. The teacher planned a trip to the school library, where all the

>>

students dove into the stacks to find books that would help them solve the mystery. After a group effort, the students determined the small "cocoon" was really the egg case of a praying mantis. With the mystery solved, the students' enthusiasm soon passed. The teacher placed the egg case on a shelf with other artifacts the students had brought in. The class went on, and the egg case was all but forgotten.

After several weeks, early one morning the students found a surprise waiting for them in their classroom. As they entered the classroom, the students quickly noticed something was different. It seemed like there was green fuzz over all the desks . . . and it was moving! Their desks, the walls, and even the ceiling were all covered by hundreds of tiny baby praying mantises! The forgotten egg case had hatched. What a surprise! The morning lesson plan quickly changed into how to capture tiny baby praying mantises—*lots* of baby praying mantises!

The moral of this great story is to always be aware of what you've got in your classroom or you too may get a show-and-tell surprise. Thankfully, it wasn't a hornet's nest!

Although these are good guidelines, there are always exceptions. You might get a goldfish that lives a month, whereas the teacher across the hall has had the same one for twenty years! Either way, the average life span of animals can be a helpful factor when making your selection.

You can use Tales From the Front Lines: Show-and-Tell Surprise! (page 53) as a springboard for students to do their own animal research. This will not only bring in a greater understanding regarding the life cycles of insects but also bring to light the fact that not all insects are the same, as the students in the story quickly discovered. Figure 3.2 is a sample lesson plan to help you get started.

Need for Care During School Breaks

For many, including me, dealing with animal care during school breaks is stressful and worrisome, so it's important to give it some thought during your selection process. If you are really concerned about finding animal care when school is closed, then certain animals are better than others. Animals that are *ectotherms* (cold blooded), such as reptiles and amphibians, have a slower metabolic rate than do the *endotherms*

> **Lesson Plan:** Is It a Mantis or a Butterfly?
>
> **Objective:** Using evidence from research, students will be able to illustrate that not all insects are the same.
>
> **Materials:** Books, databases, websites, butcher's paper, construction paper, pens, and pencils
>
> **Instructions:**
>
> 1. Students will research insects, specifically butterflies and mantises. The focus of this research should include life cycles, predators or prey, incomplete and complete metamorphosis, and the body parts that classify insects (that is, the head, thorax, abdomen).
>
> 2. Students will create a pictograph (either digitally or their own drawings or illustrations) that shows the life cycle of both a mantis and a butterfly. They should also incorporate the seasons for each part of the life cycle (for example, in the Show-and-Tell Surprise story, the egg case was found on a Christmas tree, indicating winter).
>
> 3. Students will also create a graph showing the similarities and differences of each insect. The graph should include, but not be limited to, predators, metamorphosis, food sources, how they eat (proboscis or chewing mouth), pollinators or carnivores, migration, and camouflage.
>
> **Additional Activities:**
>
> - Have students create a game that supports what they have learned about insects. Provide criteria for their game. For example, the game must have directions for the players, there must be a clear way to win, and so on.
>
> - Have students write a story about what they would have done if they had discovered the mantises in their classroom.
>
> - Have students try to persuade someone who is trying to get rid of bugs in their garden to use a mantis egg case instead of pesticides. They may choose to present this orally or in writing.
>
> **Evaluation:** Create a rubric that not only focuses on the instructional part of the lesson but also incorporates a cross-curricular identification of strengths and areas for improvement in procedural or persuasive writing with additional activities.
>
> **Additional Resources:**
>
> https://study.com/academy/lesson/praying-mantis-lesson-plan.html
>
> http://praying-mantis.org/praying-mantis-life-cycle
>
> https://www.monarch-butterfly.com

Figure 3.2: Butterfly and mantis research lesson plan.

(mammals and birds), meaning ectotherms don't have to eat as often as their warm-blooded counterparts. Ectotherms can be fantastic for the classroom because they simply do not require as much daily care, and many reptiles and amphibians don't even require daily feeding. Many snakes can be fed once every few weeks, and with adequate water, light, and heat, they can last extended periods of time with only minimal care. Many types of lizards, frogs, and toads are good candidates as well. With these types of animals, your class can place excess food like live crickets or mealworms inside the enclosure for the animal to feed on as needed, resulting in minimal human supervision over breaks; they essentially feed themselves. Conversely, animals like guinea pigs, rabbits, and birds are probably not classroom animals you want to acquire unless you have a well-thought-out plan for their care during school breaks. Their daily needs require a lot more attention, so you'll need a more detailed plan of attack when dealing with breaks. Choose wisely!

Available Space

Space is another thing to consider when selecting an animal. How much space do you have in your classroom, and how much space do particular animals require? These are important questions. Some animals require a lot of space. Some, like chameleons or iguanas, require space for climbing, whereas others, like gerbils, guinea pigs, and hamsters, need space to roam around and explore. You may simply not have enough space for some of the animals you desire. If you are short on space, a small aquarium or terrarium may be all you have room for.

Besides the actual space animals need, you will need to assess your electrical power needs in these spaces. You may have the space for a small aquarium, but do you have the electrical outlets in the right places? Many animal habitats require multiple electrical outlets for a plethora of cords. For a small aquarium, you will need a power source for a pump and filter, a light, and a heater. Even more electrical outlets can be necessary for animals with very specific heat, light, and humidity requirements. A busy classroom is no place for extension cords, so make sure you have a power source in the same space as the animal *before* it arrives!

Endangered Status

It's always a good practice before you select any animal or let any animal in your classroom to make sure it's not a protected species. Each state has its own list of protected species and the list changes frequently, so be sure to check your state's DNR website.

What makes an animal endangered? The International Union for Conservation of Nature and Natural Resources (n.d.) developed its *Red List* of criteria for classifying a species as endangered. Based on a scientific approach, the Red List judges a species on the following five standards (Dublin, 2009).

1. Population reduction rates
2. Geographic range

3. Population size
4. Population restrictions
5. Probability of extinction (in the wild)

These criteria place animals into specific categories, as table 3.1 shows. On the other hand, it is a rare and fantastic opportunity to host an endangered species in your classroom, especially if it is part of a Head Start program (see page 22 for more information on these programs). Your students can actually play an active, real-time role in that animal's survival in the wild! It doesn't get much more rewarding than that. However, this type of commitment isn't for everyone, because there is considerable paperwork involved. If you decide that this is just what you are looking for, work closely with your state's DNR and make sure you obtain all the proper permits. It can be a tricky process, but your DNR will assist you. Go for it, and make a difference!

Table 3.1: Categories of Endangered Species

Category	Definition	Example
Least Concern	A species with an abundant, widespread population	American alligator
Near Threatened	A species that could qualify as a threatened species in the near future	Gray bat (Conservation efforts helped move this species from endangered to near threatened.)
Vulnerable	A species that is likely to become endangered in the near future	Fringed dwarf mantis
Endangered	A species that has been categorized to become extinct in the near future	Chimpanzee
Critically Endangered	A species that is at an extremely high risk of extinction	Marbled gecko
Extinct in the Wild	No living members of a certain species still living in the wild	Guam rail
Extinct	No living members of a species exists	Floreana giant tortoise

Source: Adapted from Dublin, 2009; International Union for Conservation of Nature and Natural Resources, n.d.

Popular Classroom Pets

Taking all these elements into careful consideration can result in a smooth animal introduction into your classroom. By now, a certain animal may jump right out as an obvious choice, or maybe you have your heart set on one specific animal you had as a child, or maybe you are still unsure which to choose. Whatever the case may be, here is a list of great starter animals for a classroom that I can promise will not overwhelm you.

- Goldfish
- Ant farms
- Hermit crabs
- Fish
- Small rodents (mice or gerbils)
- Small snakes (like corn or garter snakes)
- Snails
- Frogs, toads
- Salamanders
- Lizards (like geckos or swifts)
- Tortoises, turtles

This list is in no way inclusive; they're simply animals I have had tremendous success with in my classrooms at various times. If my suggestions aren't right for you, a survey of over five thousand teachers (as cited in AHA, 2015) reveals the most popular classroom pets across the United States. Figure 3.3 shows the results. Selecting an animal from this list will no doubt stand you in good stead.

Conclusion

This chapter outlined several important considerations to take into account when selecting your classroom animal. This is a big decision, and not one to take lightly. If you follow the steps laid out in this chapter and take care with your choices, I am confident that you will make a great decision for you and your students. Your classroom will certainly reap the benefits of your thoughtful decision making.

Once you have decided upon the perfect animal, the next step is the fun part—actually acquiring the critter! Chapter 4 will present plentiful information relating to how to locate classroom animals.

How to Select the Perfect Animal   59

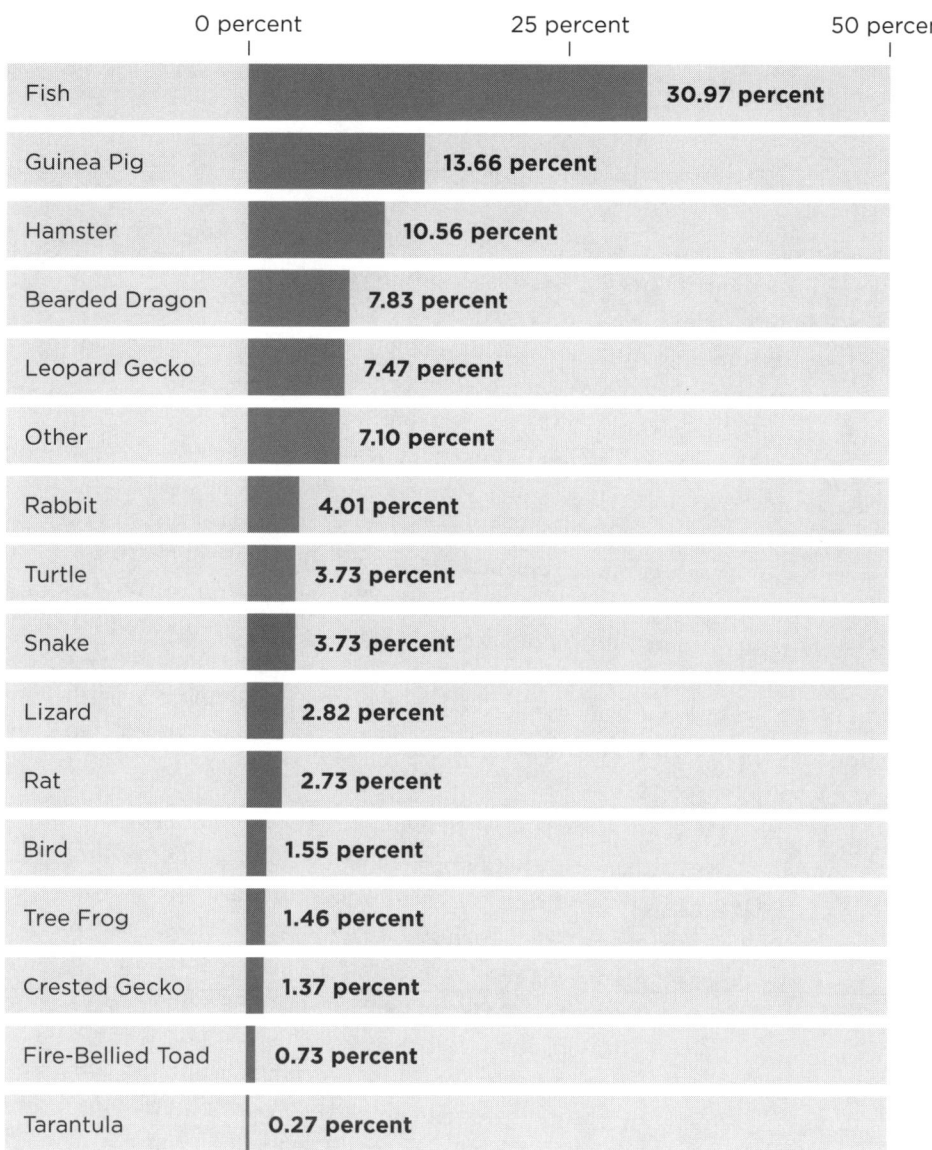

Source: American Humane Association, 2015, p. 12. Used with permission.

Figure 3.3: Survey responses to favorite type of classroom pet.

Tales From the Front Lines
Lost Leeches!

A teacher in Florida shared with me his passion for having animals in the classroom, especially animals students discovered and shared about with his class. Mr. J. told me you really don't need extra money or resources to enjoy the benefits of animals in the classroom. He encourages his students to get outside, experience nature, and interact with their world. This includes sharing what they find with the rest of the class by bringing in small critters. No, not raccoons, skunks, or crows, but rather small, capture-appropriate animals like spiders, insects, praying mantises, crayfish, and tadpoles. Mr. J. says it's a great way to generate enthusiasm, which then just seems to become infectious. The student who shares his or her find with the class is really proud, and it's up to him or her to study up on the find and teach the rest of the class all about it (for example, what kind of frog it is, where it lives, what it eats, and so on). The guest animal spends a period of time with the class and is then released back into the wild unharmed.

Mr. J., however, said it's important to know just what animal you're dealing with, especially its abilities. One time he had a student bring in a jar of leeches. He put them in a small aquarium, and the students just went bonkers over them. The students even fed the leeches raw liver and watched them swim and interact; they were just a huge hit. There was a small problem, however. The next morning, the leeches were nowhere to be found. Mr. J. wasn't aware the leech tank needed a lid—a tight-fitting one—because leeches are climbers and escape artists. At night—yes, leeches love the dark—they crawled up and out of their tank looking for their next meal. The leeches were on the loose! The students freaked out knowing there were blood-sucking leeches somewhere in their classroom, and they immediately began checking one another's arms and legs for the missing leeches. One leech was immediately located on the floor, but where were the other four? Mr. J. quickly orchestrated a search party, and all the leeches were eventually found. The moral of this story: make sure you know what your classroom animals are capable of, because you do not want to get a phone call from a parent saying he or she just found one of your lost leeches on his or her child's neck!

Brady shares a dwarf crocodile with a group of children . . . or is the crocodile sharing Dr. B?

We're going to need a bigger tank . . . how would you like to have this salamander in your classroom?

How long is the snake, a child asks . . . Well, about the length of three kids and an adult, as they found out!

To see a chameleon dramatically change colors right before your eyes is an unbelievable experience.

It never ceases to amaze me how much excitement even a simple animal, like this tortoise, can generate!

Would you rather see a picture of a kinkajou while learning about nocturnal animals, or be one of these students? Hands-on learning is everything, and their faces say it all!

Two hundred million years of reptile awesomeness preceded this encounter . . . and the student will probably remember it for just as long!

It's one thing to see an animal up close, but a whole other thing to see them in action! Here, an alligator does the dinosaur walk.

Cross-Curricular Lesson Ideas

Mathematics and Science

Have students choose four animals from the list in figure 3.3 (page 59). Students conduct research to compare the size of each animal at birth and when full grown. They then create a bar graph to illustrate the growth of each animal, as well as compare it to the others.

Note: Several animals on the chart go through metamorphosis, which would not lend itself to this lesson. However, you might choose to let students make this discovery during their research.

Science

Leeches have been used in medicine for thousands of years. Today, leeches are used as artificial veins to assist in helping restore blood flow in body parts replanted after amputation, keeping the blood flowing to help wounds heal. Older students can create a time line of how leeches have been used in medicine throughout history. It is important to highlight the various cultures that used them and why. It's fascinating stuff!

Younger students can research what leeches are and where to find them.

Science

Unfortunately, humans cause many of the factors that contribute to species endangerment. Loss of habitat due to development, pollution, and overhunting are just a few. To conserve and help with wildlife repopulation, federal and state agencies created laws for protecting endangered species. In 1973, the U.S. Congress passed the Endangered Species Act (ESA; https://fws.gov/international/laws-treaties-agreements/us-conservation-laws/endangered-species-act.html). The U.S. Fish and Wildlife Services website (FWS; www.fws.gov) shares a plethora of information about the ESA as well as links to FWS regional websites that provide information on wildlife refuges, conservation planning, tools for landowners, and more. Each region's website is specific to the animals and habitats for the states within it.

Students complete one or more of the following research activities using the FWS website.

1. Research an endangered species in your state. Include why the animal is considered endangered and what conservation plans are in place to restore the animal's habitat and numbers.
2. Research what types of conservation programs are in place where you live. Why are these programs important?
3. Interview a fish and wildlife biologist or conservation officer to learn more about what he or she does. Research what education or degree you need to become a wildlife biologist or an FWS officer.
4. Visit a wildlife refuge near you. Investigate how you can volunteer in your state or local community.
5. Schedule a virtual fieldtrip to a wildlife refuge using Skype, FaceTime, or another form of virtual communication.

Additional resources include:

- https://animallaw.info/article/state-endangered-species-chart
- https://worldwildlife.org/teaching-resources
- www.iucn.org/resources
- www.animalplanet.com/wild-animals/endangered-species
- https://nationalgeographic.org/education/resource-library/?q=endangered%20species&page=1&per_page=25

English Language Arts and Science

Have students research two or three potential classroom animals. They should investigate several topics discussed in this chapter as they relate to their chosen animals, including life span, potential for causing allergies, need for care, and space requirements. Have the students write their findings in a report and make a recommendation about which animal should be selected for your classroom.

Science

Have the students research allergies and why some animals cause allergies. As part of their research, they should investigate whether the allergy can be mitigated (by hand washing or other such methods) or not.

Mathematics
Invite students to conduct a survey of the class's favorite pets or most wished-for pets. Display the results in a bar graph or pie chart, using different colors for the different pets.

CHAPTER 4
How to Locate Animals

Now that you know which type of animal you want for your classroom, the next question is, Where do you get it? This chapter discusses a number of different options for acquiring classroom animals, including sharing, adopting, fostering, buying, and borrowing.

Sharing

This section could also be called *show-and-tell*, which was always the best part of the day for me when I was a student. Show-and-tell always took place in the morning, and anyone could stand in front of the class and share with classmates an item he or she had brought to school. It was always interesting. Some brought in stuffed animals, others fossils or feathers, but when students brought in live animals, it was off-the-chart exciting! That's usually what I brought in to share, and sometimes these animal ambassadors would stay a few days, at other times a few weeks, as guests of the class. Before returned to the wild, these animals stimulated a ton of interest, enthusiasm, and passion in all involved.

Sharing time with an animal from the wild can be one of the most rewarding situations you'll experience. To clarify, I'm not talking about encouraging students to set traps for rabbits or catch birds but rather letting students share what they have encountered on their own in the great outdoors. Encourage students to share with the class animals they come across in their backyards, on their way to school, or at their neighborhood creek. I can remember classmates bringing in everything from tadpoles to crayfish. As a kid, there were so many times when a buddy or I would capture something while walking to school (like a praying mantis or a Luna moth), and we would take it to class with us. We felt like heroes during show-and-tell on those days! Some of the greatest classroom animals I have ever experienced as a student or a teacher were ones a student or I brought in. Things like praying mantises, lightning bugs (fireflies), pill bugs (roly poly bugs), tadpoles (pollywogs), spiders, minnows, crayfish, small lizards, toads, and frogs have all found their way into my classrooms. These animals are all abundant, small, harmless, and easy to catch. They're animals that spark students' interest in nature and, for most of us, are the first animals we interact with in the wild. Most of us have caught lightning bugs on a warm spring evening, but do we really know much about them? A great thing about being a kid is becoming interested in something and wanting answers to a million new questions. Many kids (like me) will go to the library and check out a book on lightning bugs or ask lots of questions—or nowadays, check the internet for answers—anything to learn more about this fascinating creature. Students then want to share what they learn, what they discover, or what they now possess with their friends and classmates through show-and-tell.

One of my former teachers told me a large black and yellow garden spider I brought in to share was the best animal to ever visit her classroom. Garden spiders are impressively big (about the size of your ear) but completely harmless—unless you are a cricket or a moth! We kept the spider in a terrarium, where it built its web and went about its daily routine, just like it would outdoors. All the students were fascinated watching it build its web, catch and wrap up its prey, and then feed. During every recess, it became a race against the clock because, before the next bell would ring, we had to find a grasshopper or cricket for the spider's next meal. We named the spider Charlotte, of course, after the spider in the popular children's book *Charlotte's Web*. Our teacher worked the spider into dozens of lesson plans over the many weeks it shared our classroom. This spider taught us so much about life and death. Eventually, the class decided to release Charlotte back outdoors before it got too cold, so I released it back into our family garden where I had captured it. That spider facilitated many discussions between the teacher and students about life, death, eating, feeding, living, predation, arachnids versus insects, life cycles, energy, and engineering. Many of those discussions I remember even to this day. Charlotte was a rock star in our class, and she didn't cost a penny.

I strongly encourage you to let students share their small "captures" with the class, and in some instances, let the animal be an ambassador and hang around for a few weeks, teaching others all about its unique attributes and way of life. Every student should have the chance to see a tadpole turn into a frog . . . a tadpole a student hand-captured and shared with the class. That's what being a kid is all about. Please remember, after its short stay, *always* release your ambassador animal back into the wild where it was captured.

Adopting

Adopting (rather than buying) can be a great way to acquire a classroom animal. It's good for the class, and can be good for the animal. The Massachusetts Society for the Prevention of Cruelty to Animals (MSPCA-Angell, n.d.) encourages educators to adopt rather than purchase animals for their classroom because it supports the philosophy that classroom animals are a long-term commitment as opposed to a short-term belonging. Adoptions can come from many different places, like rescue centers, your local Humane Society, or your state's DNR. In my experience, I have found that local rescue centers are usually busting at the seams with injured or unwanted animals in need of homes. These agencies are very careful about where these animals end up, and they go to great lengths to ensure they find positive, safe environments for each and every one. Educators are normally viewed as good options for animal placement, so they can obtain many of the animals following a short evaluation process designed to ensure the animals are suitable for potential adopters. Your local rescue center probably isn't going to release a great horned owl to your care because it needs a lot of space and has razor-sharp talons. However, that small screech owl could work out for you. Sometimes these animals are abandoned or unwanted pets (such as rabbits, iguanas, turtles, or tortoises) that can be fantastic additions to your classroom. After a period of time, if the rescue center cannot find new homes for these animals, many will be euthanized. There's an additional incentive for getting them into your classroom—you could potentially save lives!

In other instances, the animals were never pets but injured wildlife that cannot be returned to the wild, like a box turtle hit by a car or a bird with a broken wing. These animals can no longer survive in the wild on their own and, therefore, need human assistance to survive. They usually serve out their lives in captivity as ambassadors for their species, helping to raise awareness for their wild counterparts. They are educational animals. Depending on the animal, its size or even its temperament may preclude it from being an actual hands-on animal, yet it can still be an incredible classroom addition. A good example is a screech owl—it's not something your students are going to cuddle up to, but it is an animal that nevertheless offers amazing opportunities for students to experience a little-known animal up close and personal. In addition, these injured animals can be fantastic for starting discussions and relating to students with disabilities.

Yet another source for classroom animals can be law enforcement agencies that have confiscated animals from people for illegally possessing them. The FWS and your state's DNR will often retain these animals because they cannot be returned to the wild. My local education center acquired diamondback terrapins someone was trying to smuggle out of the United States. The police apprehended the criminal at an airport trying to leave with dozens of turtles taped to his body. Sadly, these turtles were destined for the overseas black market. Since the exact location of the turtles' wild capture was unknown, these confiscated animals couldn't be released back into the wild because they could compromise the genetics of a local, naturally occurring population. Therefore, the only alternatives were to euthanize the animals or to find homes for them at zoos or other educational facilities, like my classroom. When the animals are an endangered species, euthanizing normally isn't an option, making a classroom destination ideal. Making a phone call and letting these types of agencies know you're interested in such animals and getting on their list of potential adopters can sometimes yield amazing results.

Lastly, another approach to adopting a classroom animal can be through your local DNR or state game and fish commission. In many U.S. states, these agencies provide educators animals of special concern. These are native animals that may be endangered or threatened, keystone species, or players of an important role in the health, recovery, or maintenance of local ecosystems. In my home state of Maryland, the DNR has education projects involving a wide variety of animals like eels, blue crabs, terrapins, oysters, and many others. They are all species that play important roles in the health of the Chesapeake Bay. Oftentimes, these animals are involved with head-start programs (see chapter 1, page 22, for additional information), where students raise the animals over the course of the school year and then release them back into the wild at the end of the school year. In my local schools, the Terrapin Program is the most popular with students, teachers, and parents, and the local press seems to cover it every year. Another popular head-start program around the Chesapeake Bay has been dubbed the Green Eggs & Sand Program. Middle school and high school students hatch horseshoe crab eggs (which are green) and then raise the crabs for eventual release into the wild. Horseshoe crabs have important interrelationships with other species in the ecosystem, making it a vital target species.

In other parts of the United States, teachers tell me of many similar DNR programs involving a full range of species like butterflies, tortoises, smallmouth bass, and trout that students raise in the classroom. The state of Illinois has a project whereby students raise beetles for eventual release into the wild. The beetles are not the target species, but rather *what they eat*. The beetles are important because they eat an invasive exotic plant that degrades local wetlands. Another fascinating example occurs in Arizona, where the state game and fish agency runs a project in which students build desert tortoise habitats, called *courtyard habitats*, not inside the classroom but rather outdoors on school grounds, thus allowing schools to experience animals that may not fit into, or be suitable for, indoor classroom settings. No matter the animal or geographic location, these state-run head-start programs are proven winners when it comes to raising awareness and generating passion for ecosystems across the United States.

In addition, these programs are usually all-inclusive, providing not just the animals but also the expertise for their care and all the materials needed for their well-being. What a deal! As an educator, you will be hard-pressed to find a better, cheaper, easier, or more structured way to provide your classroom with animals than through a DNR head-start program. Contact your local DNR or game and fish commission for details.

Fostering

Fostering sick animals can be a great way to get an animal into your classroom, and it is many times a much more rewarding experience for your students than purchasing an animal outright. Oftentimes, U.S. state game and fish agencies or other local authorities will seize abused or neglected animals from private owners. These animals often require a great deal of care to get them healthy and back up to speed. Nursing these sick animals can be labor-intensive, which can be a hardship for agencies already short-staffed and pressed for time. The quickest solution is to euthanize the sick animals, but this is far from the best solution. Therefore, finding individuals or education facilities like schools, learning centers, or before- and after-care businesses is a great way to save animal lives in addition to introducing young people to wildlife.

A teacher tells me that in his local community, the game commission seized a large number of lizards in very poor health. The veterinarian recommended euthanasia for the extremely emaciated lizards. Hearing this news, the teacher contacted local facilities and offered his classroom for some of the lizards, informing officials that his students, under the direction of the veterinarian, would nurse them back to health, and then return them when healthy and suitable for adoption. The game commission took him up on the offer, and his classroom got a handful of sick lizards. The plan worked out incredibly well. The teacher told me he feels like it is more rewarding for the students to care for sick animals rather than regular classroom animals, because not only do the students get to be caregivers but they must also play the role of nurses, being observant and dedicated to the sick patients. He sums it up:

> My students just loved it because they were able to learn how to medicate, tube feed, check vitals, properly examine, and monitor for signs of improvement—all much more than we do for our resident

animals, which really seemed to form a special bond between kids and the sick animals. The students were extremely happy when the lizards recovered, but also sad when they left us to go back for adoption. It was a special moment. (C. Morris, personal communication, June 20, 2018)

After hearing about these incredible results and the amazing benefits the sick animals can provide students firsthand, I highly recommend looking into the possibilities of fostering confiscated sick or mistreated animals. Contact your local or U.S. state game and fish commission or local wildlife rescue centers, and get on their list.

Buying

When buying classroom animals, proceed with caution. It's not as easy as running down to your local pet store and purchasing an animal this afternoon. When purchasing animals for your classroom, it is important to make sure you are buying from a reputable source. Purchasing from your local pet store can sometimes be risky because the animals could come from questionable sources or even from the wild. In fact, even many of the large, nationally known franchise pet stores have received negative press over the last few years for using questionable sources for acquiring their animal stock (Bowerman, 2016). The problem is some pet stores sell animals imported from places where they were illegally collected from the wild. This is definitely not a good thing because unregulated collection can wipe out natural populations and start a domino effect of negative changes to the habitat. In addition, wild-caught animals are usually in poor health and can be riddled with parasites or diseases, something you will have to deal with once they're in your hands. Their journey can be long and inhumane, and the illegal exploitation and destruction of nature is something you definitely do not want to play a role in.

It's always best to ensure your animals are coming from licensed, responsible sources. To determine this, always ask questions and look for pertinent information on company websites. Make sure dealers are using captive-bred stock for the animals they sell. When it comes to tropical aquarium fish, look for the Marine Aquarium Council seal of approval; it ensures your fish weren't being illegally captured and thus destroying populations in nature. Inquire whether the company provides a health warranty and guarantee. If your animal happens to die shortly after you receive it, you should be guaranteed a replacement. Determine whether the company stands behind its product. When available, check out customer comments and see how others feel about the company. You can never be too careful when it comes to buying live animals.

I've always found a safe and great place to buy many of my classroom animals; it can be a biological supply company like Carolina Biological Supply Company (https://carolina.com). When ordering from companies like this one, you can avoid legal and ethical issues about the source of the animals. Many of you are probably already familiar with Carolina but may not be aware they sell living organisms. Carolina provides over 5,000 different types of living plants and animals for science education classrooms across the United States. They also provide maintenance and care sheets for educators. Be sure to ask many questions when purchasing, and always look for licensed and reputable dealers when acquiring your classroom animals, and you will be doing all the right things.

Borrowing

Let's say you have a unit on the Antarctic coming up, and you're finding it difficult to get your students excited about this amazing place just by watching videos and staring at textbook photos. How about bringing a penguin into your classroom? Yes, you heard me right! There are ways to get amazing animals into your classroom—ones you could never keep full-time inside your classroom. I like to call it *borrowing an animal for an unforgettable encounter*. It's great to let students experience an animal firsthand that doesn't, or simply can't, live in your classroom; the animal may be too large, too exotic, or even too dangerous to call your classroom home. Nevertheless, when expert handlers present these types of animals, they offer outstanding educational opportunities and generate off-the-charts enthusiasm!

Education centers, zoos, and aquariums virtually all have some form of animal outreach program. These outreach programs usually go by catchy names like ZOOmobile (Maryland Zoo), Aquarium on Wheels (National Aquarium in Baltimore, Maryland), or Zoo to Do (Virginia Zoo). These programs all center on providing opportunities for students to get up close and personal in the classroom with animals they might not ever see otherwise. The animals are brought to you—animals like penguins, sloths, or eagles—all big, impressive animals that could never call your classroom home. Unfortunately, these visits usually don't come cheap. However, many facilities do offer reduced or even free programs to certain qualifying schools. Check with your local zoo, aquarium, or children's museum to see which outreach programs are available at what cost. In addition, your PTA might provide funds for these visits; in my experience, this group often pays for my visits with animals into schools.

Finally, you might want to experience an animal before you go to all the trouble of acquiring it, so borrowing can be a great option. Many outreach programs provide animals you can actually keep in your classroom, such as lizards and snakes. So, before you take the plunge to get that hedgehog or alligator, these outreach animals let you experience critters up close and in person, thus allowing you to make a more educated decision. You might learn from an outreach visit that the giant cane toad you had your heart set on urinates when it's handled, or that tarantulas will oftentimes flick tiny irritating hairs from their backs into the air and then into your eyes. Outreach visits to your classroom can be a great way to experience phenomenal creatures you simply cannot house in your classroom, but more important, they also provide a way to get a feel for which animal would make a great addition to your classroom. See what's available in your area and try a few visits.

Conclusion

As this chapter outlined, there are many places to locate your classroom animal. Some of them may not be right for you at this time or for a particular animal you seek, but things can change over time. At some point in your career you might be ready for more elaborate, time-consuming animals, or possibly even a rescued animal or an endangered species. Give careful consideration to your many options and the right avenue of acquiring your new animal will become crystal clear. It's a fun process, one that you should enjoy whether you choose to adopt, rescue, or purchase.

Once you actually have the animal in your classroom, be prepared because something magical will likely happen—you are likely to have several ideas pop into your head about how you can use your new animal in lesson plans and classroom activities! We discuss the art of incorporating classroom animals into your lesson plans in the following chapter.

Cross-Curricular Lesson Ideas

Reading and English Language Arts
Introduce your students to spiders by reading *Charlotte's Web* by E. B. White. In addition to giving information on the function of spiderwebs and life cycle of spiders, the book provides rich opportunities for discussions about character traits such as generosity, integrity, loyalty, and devotion. Older students may be interested to know that Charlotte's last name, Cavatica, comes from *Araneus cavaticus*, the scientific name for a barn spider. Students might enjoy researching the scientific names of other animals.

Science and Art
Take a field trip to a local lake, forest, beach, or mountain. Students can explore the environment to observe the living creatures that call the habitat home. Invite students to choose one of the animals or insects they observe, draw a picture of it, research facts about it, and then share that information with the class.

History and Geography
Have the students research the history of domesticated pets (in your country or around the world). Invite students to pick one animal that has been domesticated in the past and create a presentation on how that animal interacted with populations over time.

CHAPTER 5

How to Write Lesson Plans

In my opinion, once you've done the hard work of actually choosing an animal and getting it into your classroom, writing lesson plans is the easy part. In many cases, your students will automatically have questions about the animal, and these will organically lead to lesson plans in several subject areas. You can also use the impact of an animal in your classroom to create inquiry-based lessons. Of course, there are always plentiful resources online, including lesson plans for many different types of classroom animals, which I address later in this chapter. Finally, I will get you started by presenting sample lesson plans to take you and your class through the entire process of getting an animal into your classroom. These sample lesson plans involve students in all aspects of the process, prepare them for the animal and its care, and afford them greater responsibility and ownership over the critter once it arrives.

Natural Questions

Coming up with lesson plans centered on your classroom animal can start with the questions your students will naturally have about the animal. They will inevitably be interested in discovering where the animal comes from (geography); calculating how much it weighs, grows, and eats (mathematics); writing a short easy on what it would be like to be the animal (English language arts); or researching which ecosystem the animal calls home and why (science). Your students will provide the questions, and your job simply requires you to turn their questions into lesson plans. You will find these endless student questions result in a self-generating, endless source for lesson plans, and over time, you'll keep, improve, and modify the most fruitful plans.

An idea another teacher passed on to me, and one I always used in my classroom, is to have your students become the animal for a mock interview. The student must research the animal, learning as much about it as he or she can, and then try to predict what potential questions other students will ask about the animal. The rest of the class act as reporters, asking questions such as, "Where do you live?" "What do you eat?" "How long do you live?" "When do you poop?" and so on. I've always found students simply love this activity.

> "I use a few formal lesson plans connected to my classroom animals, but more frequently I use the animals informally to help infuse big concepts. For example, when discussing the effect of non-native organisms on ecosystems, I show them the marine (cane) toad, thus making the lesson more powerful."
>
> —**PAUL VANDERSTEEN,** *high school teacher, Illinois*
> *(personal communication, May 12, 2018)*

Paul Vandersteen knows that effective teaching involves stimulating senses (see text box)—and what better way to do that than with a dynamic, living, breathing creature? Gail Melson illustrates this well, in her book *Where the Wild Things Are*. She includes a note from biology instructor James Schrock, which says:

> "Seeing a real spider is more information-laden than seeing a movie of it, than a color photo, than a black and white photo, than a written description. . . . While Johnny may drift off during the spider photo or film on bee dances, everyone wakes up when you bring around a real brown recluse (spider) or visit a real honey bee colony." (Melson, 2001, p. 80)

I like to call such moments *wow moments*. It's when a lesson immediately engages all students and begins a frenzy of excitement and wonder. Once you have experienced a wow moment, you will bring out animals early and often!

Inquiry-Based Lessons

Paul Vandersteen's quote is a great example of how going beyond a traditional lesson plan can impact students' learning experiences. Science curriculum lends itself to inquiry-based learning opportunities—and what better way to promote active learning about your classroom animal than to have your students research topics about that animal or species? As the teacher and facilitator, you can pose a question about an animal that sparks interest in your students and, through their research, they can develop solutions.

Table 5.1 lists some common classroom animals and potential related topics of study. Some classroom animals provide a better scope of study topics than others.

Table 5.1: Classroom Animals and Possible Topics of Study

Animal	Topics of Study
Fish	• Geography of coral reefs • Farming and food sources • Ecosystems (including coral reefs) • Impacts of shark finning (secondary) • Job description of a marine biologist
Guinea Pig, Hamster, or Rat	• Life span • Classification • Origin • Job description of a veterinarian
Bearded Dragon or Lizard	• Life span • Classification • Origin • Ecosystems • Other reptiles in Australia (other than bearded dragons) • Job description of a herpetologist
Rabbit	• Life span • Classification • Investigation of why rabbits are considered production animals (secondary) • Job description of a veterinarian
Turtle or Tortoise	• Life span • Classification • Similarities and differences between turtles and tortoises • Conservancy • Job description of a herpetologist
Snake	• Life span • Classification • Venomous snakes • Overpopulation • Job description of a herpetologist
Bird	• Flying and flightless birds • Migration • Meaning of *avian dinosaur* • Messenger birds • Job description of an avian veterinarian

For example, using a classroom fish as a springboard for ideas, students can research the impact of shark finning on the shark population, and then collaborate with peers to generate possible solutions to end the practice. Since guinea pigs belong to a family under the mammal class (*Caviidae*) and don't live in the wild, however, it would be more difficult to find solutions to a need that impacts them beyond the classroom walls. However, you can still utilize your classroom animal to help students conceptualize topics and relate their learning to actual creatures instead of simply theorizing.

Online Resources

An online search will yield dozens and dozens of sources for lesson plans centered on classroom animals. In my opinion, there is no better source than Pets in the Classroom (www.petsintheclassroom.org/pets-in-the-classroom-teacher-lesson-plans-agreement). Before you can access the curricula, you must sign a simple agreement, which essentially says you will follow a hand-washing protocol and take care of the animals. Absolutely the best thing about these lesson plans is they are proven winners real teachers and students formulated. The Pets in the Classroom website has had an annual contest for several years where teachers submit their best lesson plans centered on classroom pets. On the website, you'll find the winning entries, in addition to all entries, broken down by grade (preK–2, 3–5, and 6–8) and categorized by the type of animal. This categorization helps you sort through the huge database of lesson plans, and results in an incredibly accessible, easy-to-use productive method to find just the right lesson plans to go with your animal and targeted grade level.

There are many other potential online sources for lesson plans, including the National Association of Biology Teachers (https://nabt.org/resource-links-animals), Education.com (https://education.com/lesson-plans), and BrainPOP Educators (https://educators.brainpop.com/lesson-planning). Browse those sources to see what is available, but for what it's worth, I have found none are easier to access and provide more and better organized plans than Pets in the Classroom. If you are short on time, this site will be your best friend.

Sample Lesson Plans for Researching, Selecting, and Adopting a Classroom Animal

Having a comprehensive plan prior to bringing an animal into your classroom is a must. Classrooms have various functions with different types of learners, and students also have different needs. It is important to identify the classroom variables that can have both positive and negative impacts on student learning and growth, as well as on the well-being of the animal. Through good planning and proper management of the classroom animal, you can incorporate learning experiences that truly impact your students and last a lifetime.

The following sample lesson plans will help you better plan for and facilitate lessons about a classroom animal. They include ideas and activities for a cross-curricular approach to project-based learning.

These lesson plans can also assist you and your students when submitting a state or federal application to obtain a specific species of animal (including endangered and threatened species). In this first example, students submit their application to the Sunshine State Animal Rescue in Florida (www.sunshinestateanimalrescue.com), but you can adapt the lessons as needed. Even if you do not need to submit an application, you will still likely find these sample lesson plans helpful, as your students will gain a better appreciation for the potential classroom animal because they will understand the parameters they must work within to acquire and maintain the animal.

Lesson 1—The Research Behind Classroom Animals

Before students may petition the Sunshine State Animal Rescue to acquire an animal, they must develop a solid plan and include it as part of the petitioning process. This means students must become very familiar with the animal they choose to bring into the classroom.

Objective

During this lesson, students research animals for their classroom. Either the students or the teacher may choose the animals to research. Students may work in groups or individually. Throughout their research, the students identify all the needs and costs related to each animal to determine which would be the best choice for their classroom.

Materials
- Books, databases, websites, pen, pencil, paper
- Figure 5.1 (page 80): Animal maintenance scale
- Figure 5.2 (page 81): Habitat cost sheet
- Figure 5.3 (page 82): Food cost sheet

1	2	3	4	5
Food and water no more than every two weeks; no habitat cleaning	Food and water weekly; biweekly habitat cleaning	Food and water daily; weekly habitat cleaning	Food and water more than once a day; weekly habitat cleaning	Food and water more than once a day; daily exercise or daily walks

The maintenance of a classroom pet can range from minimal to a whole lot! This should play a large factor in deciding which animal will work best for your classroom. The following is a list of suggested classroom animals. Using the 1–5 scale, rate the animals' maintenance requirements.

Animal	Rating	Reasons
Goldfish	2	Easy to feed; habitat requires minimal cleaning
Ant Farm	1	Very little food; no requirement for habitat cleaning
Hermit Crabs	2	Easy to feed; habitat requires minimal cleaning
Mice or Gerbils	3	Easy to feed; habitat requires weekly cleaning
Corn Snake	2	Easy to feed; habitat requires minimal cleaning
Snails	1	Very little food; no requirement for habitat cleaning
Frogs or Toads	3	Easy to feed; habitat requires weekly cleaning
Salamanders	3	Easy to feed; habitat requires weekly cleaning
Lizards	2	Easy to feed; habitat requires minimal cleaning
Tortoises or Turtles	2	Easy to feed; habitat requires minimal cleaning
Guinea Pigs	4	Enjoys fresh food and treats; habitat requires weekly cleaning

Note: There is no animal listed with a rating of 5; however, students might choose an animal that could require a lot of maintenance (for example, a dog or cat).

Figure 5.1: Animal maintenance scale.

Visit **go.SolutionTree.com/instruction** *for a free reproducible version of this figure.*

The habitat you create for your classroom animal is critical for its care and ability to thrive. You will need to purchase or source materials to provide the best environment for an animal living in your classroom. The habitat you create will provide shelter and safety for the animal while allowing students easy access for feeding and cleaning. You will not only have setup costs for creating the habitat but also the cost for maintenance and replacement items.

Animal: _____

Item Needed for Setup	Where You Will Purchase or Source Item	Cost	
Example: tank	Petco or local pet supply store	$24.99	
	My mom's collection	$0	
	Total Setup Cost:	$	
Items That Will Need Replacing	Times per Year	Cost	Total
Example: Gravel	Two	$7.50	$15.00
		Replacement Total Cost:	$

Total Setup Cost: $ _____ + Replacement Total Cost: $ _____

Total Annual Cost: $ _____

Figure 5.2: Habitat cost sheet.

*Visit **go.SolutionTree.com/instruction** for a free reproducible version of this figure.*

Animal: _____

Food costs for animals can vary drastically. You can find food for an ant farm in a kitchen. An ant farm requires very little maintenance, whereas a guinea pig may require hay and grass pellets, as well as fresh food daily to help with digestion. The frequency of feeding, as well as food costs, can play large factors in deciding which classroom animal works for you.

Food	Where You Will Purchase or Source Item	Cost
Kaytee brand guinea pig food Mealworms	Petco or local pet supply store Petco or local pet supply store (starting colony only)	$15.50 $4.99
	Total:	$

Food	Feeding Schedule	Amount of Food or Feeding	Total Amount per Week
Example: Kaytee brand guinea pig food	Two times per week	1 cup per feeding	2 cups

To calculate your total food costs, you will need a conversion chart or the internet.

Example: Guinea pig food comes in a 2-lb. bag. Based on the preceding data, the guinea pig requires 2 cups of food per week. This would be 16 oz. per week. A 2-lb. bag is 32 oz. Therefore, 2 lbs. of guinea pig food will last for two weeks.

*Estimate smaller food sources such as mealworms.

Using the preceding example:

Total Quantity of Food (package or source)	Amount per Feeding	Total Feedings per Week	Frequency for Purchasing or Sourcing Food
2 lbs. (32 oz.)	8 oz.	Two times per week	Every two weeks

Figure 5.3: Food cost sheet.

*Visit **go.SolutionTree.com/instruction** for a free reproducible version of this figure.*

Instructions

Using available research tools, students identify the following.

- Type of animal
- How they will obtain the animal (share, adopt, foster, buy, or borrow; see chapter 4, page 65)
- Life span
- Habitat requirements
- Indicators of good health
- Food costs
- Habitat costs
- Level of maintenance required
- Any permits or permissions required

Finally, students share their research and create a list of animals they believe best suited for the classroom animal.

Lesson 2—The Mission and Rationale for Having a Classroom Animal

It is important to have a clear and concise objective for how the animal will become part of your classroom environment. To integrate the classroom animal into learning, students must understand the following.

- Who is responsible for the animal
- Why this is the best animal for the classroom (This includes the animal's needs—for example, maintenance and care—as well as student needs.)
- Where the animal resides in the classroom (The classroom must have the proper space, lighting, and so on to accommodate the animal.)
- Why students want or need a classroom animal (What students expect to learn from the experience.)
- How students will provide for the needs of a classroom animal

Who Is Responsible for the Animal

The following task will help students understand who will be responsible for their classroom animal.

Objective

Working in groups, students create a system for the acquisition, care, and maintenance of the classroom animal. Students must have a plan for those responsible for the animal. This also includes how students will monitor the animal's health.

Materials

- Student research
- Paper, pens, pencils
- Chart paper
- Microsoft Word or Excel (optional)

Instructions

Students create calendars or schedules and health charts to support the following.

- Who will purchase the animal? (Example: The teacher will purchase the animal with grant money.)
- Who will feed the animal and clean the habitat? (Example: The first week of every month, group one will feed the classroom animal during lunch and group two will clean the habitat during fourth period.)
- Who will monitor the overall health of the animal? How? (Example: Every Friday, group three will examine the animal and complete the weekly health chart.)
- Who will take care of the animal during vacations? (Example: Students create an *Off-Campus Care Contract* to ensure the well-being and safety of the animal while it's away from school.)

Note: Students should use research about their animal to produce an animal health-charting system (for example, one that tracks skin color or texture, food and water intake, and so on).

Where the Animal Will Reside in the Classroom

The following task will help students understand where the animal will reside in their classroom.

Objective

Using graph paper, students map a diagram for where the classroom animal will reside.

Materials

- Graph paper
- Pencils, erasers, lined paper

Instructions

- Students measure the space where they want to place their animal's habitat to ensure there is plenty of room.
- Using graph paper, students illustrate the classroom floor plan, including all windows and doors, and then clearly identify the animal's habitat location.

What Qualities, Attributes, and Habitat Requirements Make the Best Classroom Animal

The following task will allow students to share their research-driven ideas about which animal will be best for their classroom.

Objective

Based on their studies and research, students explain which animal is best for their classroom.

Materials

- Student research
- Pens, pencils, paper
- Microsoft Word or Excel (optional)

Instructions

Based on their research, students write an expository paper on what qualities, attributes, and habitat features make the animal they chose best suited for their classroom. The explanation must be based on research and other findings (for example, classroom space). Students could use this essay for their application for permission to obtain and retain an animal in their classroom.

Why There is a Need for a Classroom Animal

The following task will help students understand why there is a compelling need for an animal in their classroom.

Objective

Students write a persuasive essay to a U.S. federal or state wildlife board about why they need an animal in their classroom.

Materials

- Research
- Pens, pencils, paper
- Microsoft Word or Excel (optional)

Instructions

- Students identify key words to use in their essay to support their reasoning.
- Students identify factors in their research to create a logical argument for a specific classroom animal.
- Students state their position clearly and write with passion.

How Students Provide for Their Classroom Animal

The following task will help students understand how they will financially provide for their classroom animal.

Objective

Using the cost sheets (see figures 5.1, 5.2, and 5.3, pages 80–82), students create a plan for taking financial responsibility to provide for the classroom animal.

Materials

- Completed cost sheets (food, habitat, maintenance)
- Pens, pencils, paper
- Websites, databases
- Microsoft Word or Excel (optional)

Instructions

- Using cost sheets from previous lessons, students determine an annual budget for the complete care of the classroom animal. This plan should include food and habitat costs plus the cost to acquire the animal.
- The budget must include the funding source and starting balance.
- Students also create a plan that includes estimated costs for veterinary care.
- The students' plan should also include the name of a reliable veterinarian experienced with the species of the classroom animal.
- Students create a plan to raise funds in case their budget falls short of needs for the year.

Lesson 3—The Application Process

At this point, students have completed the preparation required to apply and defend their reasons for obtaining a classroom animal. Using their information and plans from the previous lessons, students fill out the application. (Please note: figure 5.4 is only a sample application). Students may find they have more information than required for the application. If so, students need to determine which pieces of information are most important when filling out the application.

Objective

Students use the information they collected throughout each lesson to apply for permission to obtain a classroom animal.

Materials

- Sample animal services application application (see figure 5.4)
- All information and documents students created from previous lessons
- Pens, pencils, additional paper

SAMPLE ANIMAL SERVICES APPLICATION

Submit by: ___ / ___ / _____
Name of applicants: _____
School: _____
Classroom: _____
Animal you are applying for: _____

Please include a one-paragraph summary of your research about this animal.
_____
_____
_____
_____
_____
_____
_____
_____

Will your class use this animal for educational purposes? _____

If yes, please provide an explanation of what educational purposes the animal will serve.
_____
_____
_____
_____

Figure 5.4: Sample animal services application form.

How do you plan to acquire the animal? (circle one)

Adoption   Foster   Purchase

Other (please explain here)
_____
_____

Provide the name of the agency or business you will acquire the animal from.
_____

Please include any costs or fees associated with acquiring the animal.
_____
_____

Describe the habitat needs of the animal.
_____
_____
_____
_____

In a two-paragraph essay, explain the reasons why you are applying for the animal and why the animal services board should approve your request.
_____
_____
_____
_____
_____
_____
_____
_____
_____
_____
_____
_____
_____
_____
_____

Please attach the following.

- Habitat cost sheet
- Food cost sheet
- Plan for the space, including a floor plan (on grid paper)
- Care plan (including schedules)
- Annual budget, including costs for acquiring and maintaining the animal, initial budget and funding source, as well as any incurred costs such as veterinary care or boarding.
- Plan for monitoring the health of the animal

(For official use only)

Approved by: _____ Date: _____

Feedback or rubric:

Visit go.SolutionTree.com/instruction for a free reproducible version of this figure.

Instructions

While filling out the sample animal services application, students answer or describe the following.

- Name of the animal
- What educational purposes the animal will serve
- How the class will acquire the animal
- The animal's habitat, described in detail
- The class care plan
- The class budget

- Any veterinarian needs and costs
- The class plan for monitoring the health of the animal
- A two-paragraph essay explaining the reasons for their application *and* why the animal services board should grant the request.

Note: You may wish to create a rubric for the application process. This can provide cross-curricular feedback for students as well as allow for differentiated instruction within your groups or grade levels.

Lesson 4—Animal Elections

Now that your students have created a comprehensive plan, it is time to choose an animal. Having a class election can be a great way to share the students' information and ideas as well as to familiarize them with the election process.

Note: The teacher or a mock animal services board must approve plans before students are eligible to participate in the election process.

Objective

Students create a presentation that supports facts and reasoning for why the animal should become the classroom animal.

Materials

- Sample animal services application form (see figure 5.4, page 87)
- Presentation board or PowerPoint
- Pens, pencils, markers, crayons
- Any copies of information students want to include on their presentation board (not needed for PowerPoint)

Instructions

Students include the following on a presentation board or PowerPoint.

- Animal (including description and picture)
- One to two sentences about how they plan to acquire the animal
- Overview of habitat (illustrations or descriptive paragraph)
- Overall costs (acquisition and maintenance)
- Care plan (graphs, schedules, or descriptive paragraph). This plan must include in-class and off-campus care, as well as any possible veterinary needs.

- Paragraph or infographic explaining what they can learn from the classroom animal
- Persuasive summary of why they believe the animal is best suited to be the classroom animal

Lesson 5—Choosing a Classroom Animal

At this point, your students have put a lot of work into deciding what animal is best for the classroom. Now it is time to make a choice! This is a great opportunity to discuss a selection process. Your students (or you) may decide a democratic process and election is the best approach. Or, if that isn't what would work best for your class, your students submit their applications to a "board" (group of teachers, administrators, and so on) and go through a selection process. Either way, this is a great way to summarize what students have learned and done to bring the best animal into the classroom.

If your class participates in an election, it is important for students to respect one another's arguments during the process. After students deliver their presentations, they prepare a list of election expectations. These expectations may include, but are not limited to, the following.

- Deciding whether the election will be open or closed (hands or ballots)
- Establishing how the class will ensure the election process is fair and honest
- Agreeing on no bullying
- Establishing that everyone will respect and accept the final decision regardless of the process

Note: After students view each presentation, they may decide the animal is *not* the best choice for the classroom. This is a terrific opportunity to discuss the power of personal choice and to explain that it is acceptable to vote for an animal other than their first choice.

Additional Activities

Following are some additional activities you may want to include in the classroom animal selection process.

Social Media Star

Make your classroom animal a social media star! This is a great opportunity for students to bring awareness to the successes of having an animal in the classroom.

They will learn communication skills and internet safety. Social media can also be a great way to raise money for a cause or even your own classroom animal's care.

Career Exploration

While conducting research and developing their plan, students may choose to contact local veterinarians or zoologists. Thanks to technology like FaceTime and Skype, many organizations offer time to share the importance of what students do and how they do it. You and your students can also do the following.

- Visit your local zoo.
- Become familiar with your local animal shelters and rescue organizations (there are all kinds).
- Interview the veterinarian who takes care of your pet.
- Learn about wildlife organizations near you and how you can help.

Conclusion

There is so much to learn about having a classroom animal. The process for selecting an animal through carefully thought-out lessons and project-based learning opportunities will enrich the experience and help your learning community understand the importance of having a classroom animal and the responsibilities that go with it. The best takeaway from this experience should be that your students will acquire skills to help develop their SEL, as well as put them on their way to become animal experts!

Epilogue

Congratulations! If you made it this far, you are ready to welcome an animal into your classroom. If you follow the simple road map I have laid out for you, you should have the confidence and knowledge to successfully navigate the winding road to getting animals inside your classroom, allowing you and your students to enjoy the enormous benefits they will provide.

However, I know what many of you are probably thinking right now: that this sounds great, you know you can do this, but now might not be the right time—that you will start this process next semester or next year. My answer to you is *there is no time like the present*. When talking to teachers or parents, I see firsthand children who are, in many instances, completely devoid of hands-on experiences with animals and even with nature. I believe this situation is an emergency we, as educators, must address immediately—with animals in the classroom.

Oftentimes, when I'm talking to hesitant educators about hands-on learning with animals, I often fall back on the outstanding Louv (2005) book, *Last Child in the Woods*. Louv (2005) explains this problem so well, he makes this emergency tangible and real. We all probably agree that many children are separated in many ways from nature, but Louv (2005) really probes the reasons *why* and opens our eyes to a reality many look right past. For example, he writes of the problem, "A generation of children is not only being raised indoors, but is being confined to even smaller spaces" (Louv, 2005, p. 35). He goes on to describe how University of Maryland Professor Jane Clark dubs today's children *containerized kids* because they spend more and more time "restrained in containers" (as cited in Louv, 2015). He writes:

> They spend more and more time in car seats, high chairs, and even baby seats watching TV. . . . When small children go outside, they're often placed in containers—strollers—and pushed by walking or jogging parents. Most kid-containerizing is done for safety concerns, but the long-term health of these children is compromised. (Louv, 2008, p. 35).

I don't like the sound of containerized kids, but I must admit I did exactly this with both my children. I "containerized" them as much as possible, not really thinking much about it until much later. When these children do finally escape their containers, they have the internet, TV, tablets, smartphones, laptops, video games, and yes, even air conditioning, all to keep them isolated from the natural world. It is now natural and accepted to see an electronic device mesmerize a child on the couch. As educators, let's do our part to reverse this trend. We can, in a small way, unbox containerized kids, help put them back into nature, and help them marvel at the world surrounding them. It doesn't take much to reach these children, show them an alternative to their virtual world, and reconnect them with the natural world. Classroom animals are an easy and immediate step you can take right now to help get students back on the nature track.

If you are like me, you will find few things in your teaching career as gratifying as reconnecting—or connecting—students with nature. Remember, you might not think it's a big deal when you put that shy student in the back of your classroom in charge of the ten-gallon aquarium, but it just might be a huge deal for him or her! It sure was for me, transforming and energizing me, and setting me down on the pathway to become a National Geographic explorer. You will never know it at the time, but you and your classroom animal might just be the catalyst that sets in motion the next Jacques Cousteau, Jane Goodall, or Charles Darwin. Always believe in, embrace, and carry the torch for the classroom animal and its amazing educational abilities. You'll find the journey so rewarding. There is a place—a prominent place, always—for the classroom turtle!

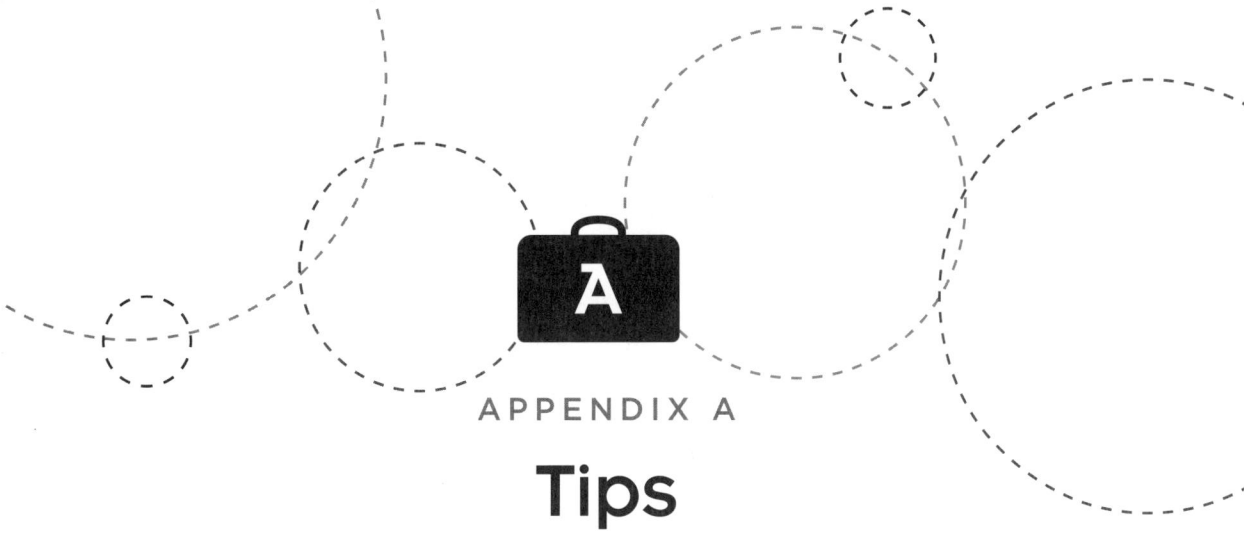

APPENDIX A

Tips

This appendix contains various tips and tricks for the care of different animals and animal groups; sourcing food; and finding, setting up, and maintaining cages and aquariums.

General Tips for Animals

Amphibians

- *Always* wash your hands with soap before handling amphibians because they have ultra-sensitive skin. Do not use hand sanitizer before you handle amphibians because the alcohol can burn the animal's sensitive skin.
- If you see your frog sitting in its water dish, don't be alarmed. Frogs drink water through their bottoms!
- Don't be hesitant to train any and all of your animals. I have seen students train animals as small as frogs to approach a feeding area and even step onto a small scale to be weighed!

Birds

- Many birds will lay eggs, even without the presence of a male.
- Provide your classroom finch a cuttlebone or mineral block to promote a healthy beak.
- Canaries and finches like to take baths, so provide a dish of water or spritz them with water to keep them clean and happy.

Reptiles

- When presenting a snake to students for a hands-on encounter, *always* control the snake's head and keep it well away from students.
- If you have mammals *and* snakes in the classroom, *never* handle the mammals before you handle a snake without first washing your hands. You don't want to make the snake mistake your hand for a meal!
- When keeping snakes, allow them access to a dish of water so they can also submerge themselves. Right before they shed, soaking helps loosen up their old skin.
- Don't be alarmed if you suddenly see your snake's eyes turning a cloudy blue. This just indicates it is going to shed its skin soon.
- Keep a rock or other rough-surfaced item inside a snake enclosure. These objects can facilitate shedding by allowing the snake to rub against it.
- Snakes have no eyelids, so you never know if they are asleep. Always use a snake hook to gently touch a snake before picking it up, thereby ensuring you don't startle it awake from a deep sleep. This will also help you avoid receiving a cranky snake bite!
- When handling lizards, *never* hold them by the tail because their tails can break off. (The tails will grow back, but the process takes many months.)
- Only feed your lizard food no longer than the distance between the lizard's eyes.
- Many reptiles will lay eggs, even without the presence of a male.
- Chameleons change their body color based on mood. After a short period of time, you will learn which color represents a happy or an angry lizard!

Small Mammals (Hamsters, Mice, Gerbils)

- *Always* provide something hard for your small mammals to gnaw on. A hard dog biscuit works well. They need to wear down their constantly growing teeth.
- Provide hamsters and gerbils with old paper towel rolls. These give them a hiding spot as well as something they can chew on.

Arachnids

- When holding a tarantula, *always* hold it over a desktop or close to the ground. Tarantulas are fragile and susceptible to literally breaking in two when dropped.
- Don't be surprised if one day you see two tarantulas in an enclosure when you only possess one. When they shed (molt), their old skin will look like an exact copy of the original spider!
- Place a black light over your scorpion enclosure and you will be amazed! Scorpions glow dramatically under black light.

Tips for Sourcing Food for Animals

- Place a piece of fruit in a jar and then leave it in a suitable location, one where you won't mind having a swarm of flies show up. This will attract fruit flies, which are a great food source for many frogs and small lizards.
- Have students catch living flies. They are a great and free food source for small lizards and frogs.
- Purchase *weekend feeders*, which include tablets that release fish food gradually over time. This can be a great way to feed your classroom fish over a long holiday weekend.
- If you have small animals that eat mealworms, it is easy to start a self-sustaining mealworm colony and save a lot of cost. (See appendix B, page 99, for more information.)
- Have your students bring in living earthworms. They make a great and free food source for many reptiles, amphibians, and fish. Students can collect earthworms on the playground after a rain when they come to the surface.
- Set up a cockroach trap around the school dumpster or other suitable site (for me it was the teachers' lounge!). This is a great way to acquire a free food source for lizards.

Tips for Finding, Setting Up, and Maintaining Cages and Aquariums

- Collect all the newspapers you can! Newspapers are great for covering the bottoms of cage enclosures.

- Use cedar wood chips as bedding for many small mammals (like guinea pigs and hamsters). It's a great way to add a pleasant odor to your classroom and mask any animal odor.
- Don't throw that old, cracked aquarium away! Even if an aquarium won't hold water, it can make a great terrarium or habitat for small terrestrial animals. Garage sales are great places to find old aquariums.
- Include an algae-eating suckermouth catfish (pleco) in every aquarium to help keep the glass nice and clean.
- Conduct periodic partial water changes in your aquariums. This will help keep them healthy and clean.
- Try putting all your animal enclosure lights on electrical timers. This way, you don't have to remember to turn them on and off.
- Don't cook your animals! Always have a temperature gradient across the enclosure. Place your heater or basking lamp on one side of the cage to keep it warm, but let the other side stay cool.
- Avoid using aerosol air fresheners near amphibian enclosures. They can be problematic for the animals' thin, sensitive skin.
- *Never* use water straight from the tap in an aquarium. It is treated with a number of chemicals that can harm fish. Well water can safely be used, as can distilled water or even rainwater—just let it sit for forty-eight hours before using. Commercially made liquid water containers, found at pet stores, may be the easiest solution.
- A solution of diluted vinegar and water makes a great, safe animal habitat cleaner.
- Live plants in a classroom aquarium can be difficult to maintain. Consider using artificial plants to minimize tank maintenance.
- Never leave fruits or vegetables inside an animal enclosure for more than a day or you will get an unwanted swarm of fruit flies!

APPENDIX B

How to Create Self-Sustaining Food Sources for Your Classroom Animal

This appendix contains various tips and tricks for creating self-sustaining food sources for your classroom animals, specifically, fruit fly and mealworm colonies.

How to Start a Fruit Fly Colony

Starting a fruit fly (Drosophila) colony is super easy and will provide your hungry classroom critters with lots of tasty fruit-fly goodness. Many small classroom animals require tiny prey like fruit flies, particularly lizards, frogs, toads, spiders, and even insects like praying mantises. In addition, your class can use living fruit flies in dozens of various lessons and experiments. A quick internet search will yield more lesson plans involving fruit flies than you could ever hope to use. Here's how you can get started on your own fruit fly colony.

Supplies

- Fruit fly stock (from local pet store or online)
- One 16 oz. or 32 oz. plastic cup with a tight-fitting lid (deli containers work best)
- One water bottle lid
- Sharp scissors
- Tissue, coffee filters, or dryer sheets

- One can of beer
- One small box of instant mashed potato flakes
- One small bottle of white vinegar
- One package of dry yeast
- Shredded paper

To begin the wonderful world of growing fruit flies, you will need *starter stock*, that is, living fruit flies. I highly recommend locating flightless fruit flies for your starter stock. These are genetically mutated flies that cannot fly, and that's *important*. It's critical because it's easier for your animals to capture and eat the flightless fruit flies, but more important, it makes the fruit flies less likely to escape. You will invariably have some escapees, and the last thing you want in your classroom are liberated fruit flies buzzing around. Once loose, fruit flies are almost impossible to catch. You can grow and use regular old fruit flies, but believe me, you are better served tracking down some flightless ones! Flightless fruit flies are not hard to find; you can usually find them at your local pet store or order them online and receive them through the mail.

Instructions

Once you receive your starter group of fruit flies, you'll need something for them to call home. Small plastic containers work well (the kind for leftover food). You can find them at your local grocery store; restaurant carry-out food containers (the round type with a lid) work well too, and they are free!

Preparing the Fruit Fly Container

1. Draw a circle with a 1-inch diameter (tracing a water bottle lid works well) in the center of the container lid.
2. Next, cut out the circle to create an opening in the top of your container lid.
3. Cut a piece of tissue, dryer sheet, or coffee filter (twice the size of your opening) and securely tape it to the lid. These tiny guys have to breathe, but you also need to keep them in the container where they belong.

Mixing Up a Medium

You're now ready to make the food. This is the fun part!

1. Pour 8 oz. of beer into a medium-sized mixing bowl.
2. Add 8 tablespoons of potato flakes and stir.

3. Next, add 2 oz. (60 ml) of white vinegar.
4. Stir until your mixture has the consistency of a smoothie. (Resist the urge to drink it!) Note: If it is too watery, add about a teaspoon of potato flakes to reach the correct consistency.
5. Finally, add ½ teaspoon of yeast and stir well.

Your fruit-fly food is now complete and ready for you to place into the bottom of your prepared container.

1. Place 1 inch of the "fly brew" into the bottom of your container. You don't need much!
2. Add some very thin strips of paper (the kind fragile glass might be packed in) above the brew, or wad up a coffee filter and place it inside your container. This gives the flies a place to live and walk around on, so they don't drown in their own food.

Adding the Fruit Flies!

Now you can add your fruit fly stock. This can be much trickier if you have flying fruit flies. First, remove the lid from your starter stock, invert it over your brew container, and give it a series of light taps and shakes until you get approximately fifty flies into your brew container. Then, quickly place the lid on your container, and you are good to go!

If you have flies left over, use them as food or start as many colonies as you wish. Keep the colony in a warm place (room temperature is usually adequate), and sit back and relax. The flies will immediately start eating, as well as laying their eggs in the beer brew (medium). After a few days, you might see tiny little maggots worming around in the medium, and in little over a week, you will begin to see baby fruit flies. Your self-sustaining fruit fly colony is now up and running. Just think about the money you are saving!

Additional Resources

https://keepinginsects.com/general-care/breeding-fruit-flies

https://depts.washington.edu/cberglab/wordpress/outreach/an-introduction-to-fruit-flies

How to Start a Mealworm Colony

If your classroom animal requires something a little heartier than fruit flies, you can always create your own stock of mealworms. *Mealworms* are the larvae of darkling beetles and provide a great source of protein for animals such as larger lizards, turtles, frogs, chickens, and some birds. Just like fruit flies, mealworms can be costly to purchase over time, so you may choose to offset this cost by creating your own mealworm farm. Store-bought mealworms might also lack nutrients due to poor growing conditions or age. So, here's how you can harvest your own.

Supplies

- Mealworms (you can obtain an initial supply from any pet store or biological supply house)
- Plastic shoebox with lid
- Sharp scissors
- Ground oatmeal or cornmeal (You can also use dog food or even grain cereal.)
- Sliced vegetables or fruit (Potatoes are best because they take longer to dehydrate and mold.)

Instructions: Preparing Your Substrate

In biology, a *substrate* is the surface on which an organism lives. In this case, your substrate is the oatmeal, cornmeal, or other grain you add to the container.

1. Using sharp scissors, puncture the top of the container and create three rows of three small holes. Make your holes toward the top portion of each end of the box to help with air flow. You need good ventilation to prevent too much humidity and molding.
2. Add your oatmeal or cornmeal. (You can also include other items such as dog food or grain cereals.)
3. Place two to three pieces of sliced vegetables or fruit (roughly one-fourth of a small apple) on top of the substrate. This will be the mealworms' water source. Avoid the desire to include a water container; the mealworms will drown in the water.
4. Add your mealworms.
5. Keep your mealworm colony in a dark area with a temperature between seventy-five and eighty degrees.

Maintenance and Care

- Most classroom pets eat mealworms in the larvae stage of their life cycle (before they become a pupa and, eventually, a darkling beetle). If your mealworms are growing through the life cycle at a faster pace than needed (meaning you are getting more beetles than you want), place the container in a refrigerator to slow down the process.

- Remove any dead mealworms, pupa, or beetles from your container.
- If the mealworm container develops an odor that smells like ammonia, remove the mealworms (pupa and beetles too) and throw away the substrate. Then, thoroughly clean the container and add a new substrate.
- You might want to have an additional container to continue your colony by moving the beetles to a new container (set it up exactly as you did with the original). Move any remaining mealworms from the first container into the second container. Discard everything from the first container, clean it, and set it up to repeat the cycle.

Additional Resources

- http://mealwormcare.org/breeding
- www.fossweb.com/mealworm

References and Resources

American Humane Association. (2015, July). *Pets in the classroom study: Phase I findings report*. Accessed at https://americanhumane.org/app/uploads/2016/08/PETS-IN-THE-CLASSROOM-CKT-R4.pdf#page=12&zoom=auto,-74,536 on November 29, 2018.

American Humane. (n.d.). *First to serve*. Accessed at https://americanhumane.org/about-us on October 16, 2019.

Arcken, M. M. (1989). Environmental education, children, and animals. *Anthrozoös*, *3*(1), 14–19.

Bajak, A. (2014). Lectures aren't just boring, they're ineffective too, study finds. Accessed at www.sciencemag.org/news/2014/05/lectures-arent-just-boring-theyre-ineffective-too-study-finds on January 18, 2020.

Beetz, A., Uvnäs-Moberg, K., Julius, H., & Kotrschal, K. (2012). Psychosocial and psychophysiological effects of human-animal interactions: The possible role of oxytocin. *Frontiers in Psychology*, *3*, 1–15. Accessed at https://ncbi.nlm.nih.gov/pmc/articles/PMC3408111 on November 29, 2018.

Blamford, A., Clegg, L., Coulson, T., & Taylor, J. (2002). Why conservationists should heed Pokémon. *Science*, *295*(5564), 2367.

Blue, G. F. (1986). The value of pets in children's lives. *Childhood Education*, *63*(2), 84–90.

Bowerman, M. (2016, Jan 21). Petco drops animal supplier amid federal probe. *USA Today*. Accessed at https://usatoday.com/story/news/nation-now/2016/01/21/petco-peta-animal-abuse-small-animal-supplier-federal/79105326 on October 14, 2019.

Bueche, S. (2003). Going to the dogs: Therapy dogs promote reading. *Reading Today*, *20*(4), 46.

The Butterfly Site. (n.d.). *Butterfly life cycle*. Accessed at https://thebutterflysite.com/22-butterfly-coloring-pages.html on October 12, 2019.

Centers for Disease Control and Prevention. (n.d.a). *Healthy pets, healthy people*. Accessed at https://cdc.gov/healthypets/health-benefits/index.html?CDC_AA_refVal=https%3A%2F%2Fwww.cdc.gov%2Ffeatures%2Fhealthypets%2Findex.html on November 29, 2018.

Centers for Disease Control and Prevention. (n.d.b). *When and how to wash your hands.* Accessed at https://cdc.gov/handwashing/when-how-handwashing.html on October 17, 2018.

Centers for Disease Control and Prevention. (n.d.c). *When and how to use hand sanitizer.* Accessed at https://www.cdc.gov/handwashing/show-me-the-science-hand-sanitizer.html on January 17, 2020.

Daly, B., & Suggs, S. (2010). Teachers' experiences with humane education and animals in the elementary classroom: Implications for empathy development. *Journal of Moral Education, 39*(1), 101–112.

Dublin, H. (2009). IUCN Red List of threatened species. *Encyclopedia Britannica.* Accessed at https://britannica.com/topic/IUCN-Red-List-of-Threatened-Species on October 14, 2019.

Fine, A. (Ed.). (2010). *Handbook of animal assisted therapy: Theoretical foundations and guidelines for practice* (3rd ed.). San Diego, CA: Elsevier.

Fisicaro, K. (2017, October 28). Classroom pets are out in Redmond: Redmond School District updates practice to match policy, bans most animals. *Bulletin.* Accessed at https://bendbulletin.com/localstate/5704065-151/classroom-pets-are-out-in-redmond on October 14, 2019.

Freeman, S., Eddy, S. L, McDonough, M., Smith, M. K., Okoroafor, N., Jordt, H., & Wenderoth, M. P. (2014, June 10). Active learning increases student performance in science, engineering, and mathematics. *Proceedings of the National Academy of Sciences of the United States of America, 111*(23). Accessed at www.pnas.org/content/111/23/8410 on January 17, 2020.

Futterman, L. (2015, October 27). Beyond the classroom: Animals in the classroom? An ongoing debate. *Miami Herald.* Accessed at https://miamiherald.com/news/local/community/miami-dade/community-voices/article41198466.html on October 10, 2019.

Gee, N. R., Griffin, J. A., & McCardle, P. (2017). Human-animal interaction research in school settings: Current knowledge and future directions. *AERA Open, 3*(3). Accessed at https://journals.sagepub.com/doi/full/10.1177/2332858417724346 on October 12, 2019.

Gerstein, J. (2016, December 23). The imperative of experiential and hands-on learning. *User Generated Education.* Accessed at https://usergeneratededucation.wordpress.com/2016/12/23/the-imperative-of-experiential-and-hands-on-learning/ on January 17, 2020.

Goobler, D. (2019, January 15). 'Is it ever OK to lecture?' *The Chronicle of Higher Education.* Accessed at www.chronicle.com/article/Is-It-Ever-OK-to/245458 on January 17, 2020.

Hanson, T., Brooks, T. M., Da Fonseca, G. A. G., Hoffman, M., Lamoreux, J. F., Machlis, G., et al. (2009). Warfare in biodiversity hotspots. *Society for Conservation Biology, 23*(3), 578–587. Accessed at https://conbio.onlinelibrary.wiley.com/doi/full/10.1111/j.1523-1739.2009.01166.x on October 16, 2019.

Herbert, S., & Lynch, J. (2017). Classroom animals provide more than just science education. *Science & Education, 26*, 107–123.

International Union for Conservation of Nature and Natural Resources. (n.d.). *The IUCN Red List of threatened species*. Accessed at https://iucnredlist.org on October 14, 2019.

Kendrick, M. (2016, February 12). Class pets banned from Colorado preschools, schools fight back. *New 99.1 Country*. Accessed at https://k99.com/class-pets-banned-from-colorado-preschools-schools-fight-back on October 14, 2018.

Louv, R. (2005). *Last child in the woods: Saving our children from nature-deficit disorder*. Chapel Hill, NC: Alqonquin Books.

Mars Petcare U.S. (2017, August 29). Classroom pets aren't just for fun: New research reveals animals' positive impact on students. *PR Newswire*. Accessed at https://prnewswire.com/news-releases/classroom-pets-arent-just-for-fun-new-research-reveals-animals-positive-impact-on-students-300510881.html on October 14, 2019.

Martinko, K. (2016, March 25). Children spend less time outside than prison inmates. *TreeHugger*. Accessed at www.treehugger.com/culture/children-spend-less-time-outside-prison-inmates.html on October 10, 2019.

Massachusetts Society for the Prevention of Cruelty to Animals (MSPCA)-Angell. (n.d.). *Classroom pets: The humane way*. Accessed at https://mspca.org/cruelty_prevention/classroom-pets-the-humane-way-2 on October 2, 2019.

McCardle, P., McCune, S., Griffin, J. A., Esposito, L., & Freund, L. S. (2011). *Animals in our lives: Human-animal interaction in family, community, & therapeutic settings*. Baltimore, MD: Brookes.

Melson, G. F. (2001). *Why the wild things are: Animals in the lives of children*. Cambridge, MA: Harvard University Press.

National Association of Biology Teachers. (n.d.). *Welcome to NABT*. Accessed at https://NABT.org on October 14, 2019.

National Association of Biology Teachers Board of Directors. (2019). NABT position statement: The use of animals in the biology education. *National Association of Biology Teachers*. Accessed at https://nabt.org/files/galleries/NABT_Position_Statement_Animals_in_Bio_Education-0001.pdf on January 17, 2020.

National Research Council. (1996). *National science education standards: Observe, interact, change, learn*. Washington, DC: National Academy Press. Accessed at https://nap.edu/read/4962/chapter/1 on October 15, 2019.

National Science Teachers Association. (1991). *Guidelines for responsible use of animals in the classroom: The National Science Teachers Association position statement.* Accessed at http://kindernature.org/wp-content/uploads/2017/03/Guidelines-for-Responsible-Use-of-Animals-in-the-Classroom.pdf on October 10, 2019.

National Science Teaching Association. (2008). *NSTA position statement: Responsible use of live animals and dissection in the science classroom.* Accessed at www.nsta.org/about/positions/animals.aspx on October 12, 2019.

Newlin, B. R. (2003). Paws for reading: An innovative program uses dogs to help kids read better. *School Library Journal, 49*(6), 43.

NGSS Lead States. (2013). *Next Generation Science Standards: For states, by states.* Washington, DC: National Academies Press.

Ormerod, E. J., Edney, A. T. B., Foster, S. J., & Whyman, M. C. (2005). Therapeutic applications of the human-companion animal bond. *Veterinary Record, 157*(22), 689–691.

Pets in the Classroom. (n.d.). *Grief in the classroom: How to handle the death of a classroom pet.* Accessed at www.petsintheclassroom.org/how-to-handle-the-death-of-a-classroom-pet on October 24, 2019.

Pets in the Classroom. (2014, October 28). *Pets in the classroom program provides 50,000 classrooms with educational grants.* Accessed at https://petsintheclassroom.org/pets-in-the-classroom-program-provides-50000-classrooms-with-educational-grants on October 14, 2019.

Pets in the Classroom. (2016). *Classroom pets help students with autism and emotional/behavioral issues.* Accessed at www.petsintheclassroom.org/classroom-pets-help-students-with-autism-and-emotionalbehavioral-issues/ on May 17, 2016.

Poth, R. D. (2018). Working with special needs students: What do all teachers need to know? *Getting Smart.* Accessed at www.gettingsmart.com/2018/04/working-with-special-needs-students-what-do-all-teachers-need-to-know/ on January 17, 2020.

Raupp, D. C. (2002). The "furry ceiling": Clinical psychology and human-animal studies. *Society and Animals, 10*(4), 353–358.

Ross, R. (2016, November 30). Getting clean: The science of soap. *Live Science.* Accessed at www.livescience.com/57044-science-of-soap.html on January 17, 2020.

Sack, J. L. (2003). Teachers' pets are not everybody's favorites. *Education Week, 22*(39), 5.

Semrud-Clikeman, M. (n.d.). Research in brain function and learning: The importance of matching instruction to a child's maturity level. *American Psychological Association.* Accessed at www.apa.org/education/k12/brain-function on January 17, 2020.

Smith, R., & Bowater, D. (2012, April 27). Toddlers prefer live animals to toys: Research. *Telegraph*. Accessed at https://telegraph.co.uk/news/health/news/9228729/Toddlers-prefer-live-animals-to-toys-research.html on October 14, 2019.

Soap History. (n.d.). History of soap and soap interesting facts. *Soap History*. Accessed at www.soaphistory.net on October 21, 2019.

Willis, J. (2015, November 21). How the brain works and how students can respond. *TeachThought*. Accessed at www.teachthought.com/learning/how-the-brain-works-and-how-students-can-respond/ on January 17, 2020.

Index

A
active learning methods, 12–13
adopting animals, 67–69
allergies, 41–42, 51, 52
American Humane Association, 27–28, 34, 46
amphibians, 95
amygdala, 12–13
animal care, 31–34, 35
    during vacations and breaks, 34–37, 54–56
application process, 86–90
aquariums, 1–4, 71–72, 97–98
art, 25, 73
attendance, 18
axolotls, 10–11, 21

B
Bajak, A, 12
barriers. *See* obstacles
behavioral issues, 14–16, 44
biological supply companies, 71
birds, 77, 95
Bolanos, J., 22–23
borrowing animals, 36, 65–66, 71–72
BrainPOP Educators, 78
Bruchac, J., 46
bullying, 20–21
buying animals, 70–71

C
calming effects, 9, 14–15
career exploration, 92
Carmichael, R., 9
Carolina Biological Supply Company, 71
CDC. *See* Centers for Disease Control and Prevention (CDC)
Centers for Disease Control and Prevention (CDC), 42
Charlotte's Web (White), 73
Clark, J., 93
classroom animals, 1–5
    benefits of, 8–25
    benefits outside the classroom, 18–21
    borrowing, 36, 65–66, 71–72
    classroom benefits of, 8–17
    locating, 65–73
    need for, 7–8, 85–86
    obstacles to, 27–47
    popular, 58, 59
    real-world benefits of, 22–23
    selecting, 49–63
    student interactions with, 37–40
    tips on, 95–98
cleaning, 32–33
collaboration, 19
community connections, 18
    animal care during vacations and breaks, 37
    for borrowing animals, 36, 65–66, 71–72
    for funding, 30–31
compassion, 15, 18–21
confiscated animals, 67–69
containerized kids, 93–94
cost, 29–31
    food, 82
    habitat, 81
    students and, 86

courtyard habitats, 68–69
crocodile Head Start program, 22–23
cultural issues, 42, 44, 51

D

death and illness of animals, 52–54
decision making, 19
Departments of Natural Resources (DNR), 30, 50, 57, 67, 68–69, 85–86
disabilities, students with, 10–11, 21
DNR. *See* Departments of Natural Resources (DNR)

E

Eco Adventures, 16–17, 37
ectotherms, 32, 54–56
Education.com, 78
elections, animal, 90–91
emotional needs, 9–11
empathy, 15, 18–21
endangered species, 56–57, 61–62, 68, 79
    head-start programs for, 22–23
endotherms, 54–56
engagement, 11–13, 15
    with animals, rules for, 37–41
English language arts, 46–47, 62, 73
experiential learning, 12

F

FDA. *See* U.S. Food and Drug Administration (FDA)
fish, 77
food and feeding
    cost of, 31, 82
    during school breaks, 34–37, 54–56
    self-sustaining sources for, 99–103
    sourcing, 97
fostering animals, 69–70
frogs, 20–21
fruit flies, 31, 99–101
funding, 29–31

G

geography, 25, 73
gerbils, 96
goal setting, 19
grants, 29–30
Green Eggs & Sand Program, 68
Guidelines for Responsible Use of Animals in the Classroom (NSTA), 13
guinea pigs, 77

H

habitats, 81, 85, 97–98
hamsters, 77, 96
hand sanitizers, 43
hand washing, 5, 34, 38, 95
    how to perform, 42, 43
hands-on learning, 11–13
Head Start programs, 22–23, 57, 68
health issues, 4–5, 34, 38, 41–42
    allergies, 41–42, 51, 52
hedgehogs, 39
history, 73
home stays of animals, 36–37
How the Chipmunk Got Its Stripes (Bruchac), 46
hydrophilic, 43
hydrophobic, 43

I

IFWC (inspect, feed, water, clean), 32–33
immune systems, 18
information retention, 12–13
injured animals, 67–69
inquiry-based lessons, 76–78
International Union for Conservation of Nature and Natural Resources, 56–57
interviews, mock, 75–76

J

Johnston, J., 51

K

keystone species, 22–23
kindness curricula, 20
kinesthetic learning, 12

L

Last Child in the Woods (Louv), 7, 93
leadership, 15

learning
    active, 12–13
    as fun, 15–16
    social and emotional, 18–19
leeches, 60, 61
legal issues, 49
lesson ideas, 25, 46–47, 55, 61–63, 73
lesson plans, 75–92
    inquiry-based lessons, 76–78
    natural questions for, 75–76
    online resources for, 78
    for researching, selecting, adopting animals, 78–92
liability issues, 40–41
life span, 52–54
lightning bugs, 66
limb regeneration, 10–11, 21
lipophilic, 43
lizards, 31, 38, 52, 58, 69–70, 77, 96
loaner animals, 36, 65–66
Louv, R., 7, 93

M

maintenance, 31. *See also* food and feeding
    daily animal care, 31–34
    scale on, 80
    tips for, 95–98
Martinko, K., 7
Massachusetts Society for the Prevention of Cruelty to Animals, 67
mathematics, 46, 61, 63
mealworms, 31, 101–103
Melson, G., 20, 76
mice, 96
Morris, C., 16, 30, 44
multidisciplinary engagement, 12–13. *See also* cross-curricular lesson ideas
music, 46

N

National Association of Biology Teachers (NABT), 14, 50, 78
National Geographic Society, 1–2
National Science Education Standards (NSES), 13–14

National Science Teachers Association (NSTA), 13–14, 49
nature
    affinity for animals, 8–9
    contact with, 7–8, 93–94
NSTA. *See* National Science Teachers Association (NSTA)

O

objectives, 83–86
obstacles, 27–47
    animal care during breaks and vacations, 34–37, 54–56
    cost, 29–31
    cultural issues, 42, 44
    daily care, 31–34
    health concerns, 41–42
    liability and safety issues, 40–41
    student interactions with animals, 37–40
    teacher work overload, 44–45
online resources, 78
outdoors, time spent, 7–8

P

parents
    health information from, 51, 52
    permission from, 37
Pet Care Trust, 29
Pets in the Classroom, 29, 53, 78
photography, 25
Porche, J., 9–11
praying mantises, 53–54, 55

R

rabbits, 77
rats, 77
reading, 46, 73
record keeping, 32, 34, 35
Red List, 56–57
regeneration, 10–11, 21
regulations, 49–50
relationship skills, 19
research, 54
respect, 15, 18–21
responsibility, 15, 83–84

Responsible Use of Live Animals and Dissection in the Science Classroom (NSTA), 49
Ritter, P., 13, 41
Rosnick, J., 8
Rubin, S., 14

S

safety issues, 40–41
salamanders, 10–11, 21
Salmonella, 4–5, 38, 42
school breaks, 34–37, 54–56, 84
Schrock, J., 76
science, 25, 61–63, 73
SEL. *See* social and emotional learning (SEL)
selection of animals, 49–63, 91
    age appropriateness, 51–52
    allergies, 51, 52
    care during school breaks, 54–56
    elections for, 90–91
    endangered status, 56–57
    lesson plans for, 78–92
    life span, 52–54
    popular pets, 58, 59
    space considerations, 56
    student preferences, 50
self-awareness, 19
sensory stimulation, 76
sharing animals, 36, 65–66
show-and-tell, 53–54, 65–66
sick animals, 52–54, 69–70
snakes, 38–39, 42, 44, 55–56, 77, 96
soap, 43. *See also* hand washing
social and emotional learning (SEL), 18–19, 46
social awareness, 19
social interaction, 9–11
social media star, 91–92
social studies and civics, 25, 46
sources for animals, 65–73
space considerations, 56
special needs, students with, 9–11
spiders, 39–40, 66, 73, 97
standards, 13–14
stress relief, 14–15
students
    animal costs and, 86
    in animal selection, 50
    with disabilities, 10–11, 21
    as helpers/caretakers, 44–45
    interactions of with animals, 37–40
    with special needs, 9–11
Sunshine State Animal Rescue, 79

T

tarantulas, 39–40, 97
teacher work overload, 44–45
technology, 46
touching, 38
Turtle's Race With Beaver (Bruchac), 46
turtles, 4–5, 16–17, 23, 33–34, 68–69, 77
two-finger touch, 38

U

U.S. Census Bureau, 7
U.S. Fish and Wildlife Services, 61–62
U.S. Food and Drug Administration (FDA), 4

V

vacations, 34–37, 54–56, 84
Vandersteen, P., 76

W

WALTHAM study, 18
war, 25
Where the Wild Things Are: Animals in the Lives of Children (Melson), 20, 76
White, E. B., 73
wine bottle hold, 38–39
wow moments, 76

Z

zoos, 71–72

Loving What They Learn
Alexander McNeece
Deep learning and high engagement are possible for all students, regardless of subject, grade, or previous experience. With *Loving What They Learn*, you will discover how to quantifiably measure students' needs, help strengthen their academic self-concept, and increase their self-efficacy.
BKF917

Owning It
Alex Kajitani
Today's fast-changing culture presents a great challenge—and a great opportunity—in schools and in the teaching profession. With *Owning It*, you will discover an array of easy-to-implement strategies designed to help you excel in your classroom, at your school, and in your community.
BKF835

EMPOWER Your Students
Lauren Porosoff and Jonathan Weinstein
Discover how to use the elements of EMPOWER—exploration, motivation, participation, openness, willingness, empathy, and resilience—to make school a positive, meaningful experience in your students' lives. This highly practical resource offers engaging classroom activities and strategies for incorporating student values into curriculum.
BKF791

Ready to Learn
Peg Grafwallner
Ready to Learn introduces the FRAME model, a teacher-approved approach for creating meaningful and motivating learning experiences for all students. Rely on the model's five steps to help you launch engaging lessons, articulate clear expectations, and offer effective feedback.
BKF922

Solution Tree | Press
a division of Solution Tree

Visit SolutionTree.com or call 800.733.6786 to order.

GLOBAL PD

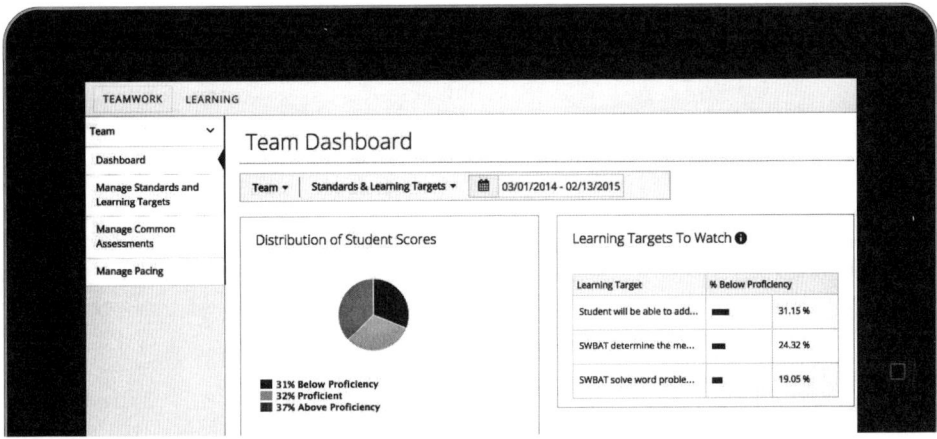

The **Power to Improve** Is in Your Hands

Global PD gives educators focused and goals-oriented training from top experts. You can rely on this innovative online tool to improve instruction in every classroom.

- Get unlimited, on-demand access to guided video and book content from top Solution Tree authors.
- Improve practices with personalized virtual coaching from PLC-certified trainers.
- Customize learning based on skill level and time commitments.

▶ **REQUEST A FREE DEMO TODAY**
SolutionTree.com/GlobalPD